Praise for Morning Reflections

*A Collection of Bible Verses, Prayers, and
Inspirational Poetry for Daily Reflection*
Hood Inspirational Reflection Series – Book 1

…"I have had this book for several weeks now, and have thoroughly enjoyed waking up to its peaceful and uplifting devotionals. Each page features a Bible verse followed by one of Hood's original poems, with a brief but insightful prayer completing the day's reading. The devotionals are centered around themes that are reflected in verse, poem, and prayer alike, and this allows the reader to really concentrate on the message and internalize it. The poems are simple yet poignant, a powerful and often elegant contemplation of various facets of the Christian walk.

I have found that my mornings tend to start much more smoothly when I set aside the time to quietly reflect on God, and Karen Hood's gentle, thoughtful words make it easy and enjoyable to do just that."…

Kim Saunders

…"**Morning Reflections**, this delightful and insightful poetry and scriptural book has proved to be a inspiration and is creatively witty with the use of heartfelt prayers and spiritual poems. It was a delight to read and I recommend this book to all who enjoy and read poetry and prayer books this is truly a book for all ages."…

Mary Scripture-Smith
Graphic Designer

Praise for Morning Reflections

A Collection of Bible Verses, Prayers, and
Inspirational Poetry for Daily Reflection
Hood Inspirational Reflection Series – Book 1

… "**Morning Reflections** evokes an awakening of the inner-self. Karen Hood's prayers and poetry are both eloquent and enlightening. Her words have the ability to transport readers to places of ponder, tranquility and inspiration. You don't have to be a scholar to appreciate the depth of character, atmosphere and emotion that emerges from these pages."…

Kimberly Carter
Spokane, WA

… "Just as each of us has a favorite comfort food, this volume of poetry is comfort food for the human spirit. The poet relates simple memories in a way that the reader can vividly experience. She is both thoughtful and thought provoking. Her poetry is naturally relaxing and a powerful community action stimulant. I find myself going back again and again to this book."…

Dr. James G. Hood
Editor

Morning Reflections

A Collection of Bible Verses, Prayers, and Inspirational Poetry for Daily Reflection

Hood Inspirational Reflection Series – Book 1

Karen Jean Matsko Hood

Current and Future Christian Books
by Karen Jean Matsko Hood

CHRISTIAN/INSPIRATIONAL/SPIRITUAL FICTION FOR ADULTS
Reflection Series

Morning Reflections – Book 1
Evening Reflections – Book 2
Reflections for Women – Book 3

CHRISTIAN/INSPIRATIONAL/SPIRITUAL NONFICTION BOOKS FOR ADULTS
Cookbooks – Christian Edition

Apple Delights – Christian Edition

CHRISTIAN/INSPIRATIONAL FICTION BOOKS FOR YOUNG ADULTS AND TEENS
Reflection Series

Reflections for Teenagers – Christian Edition

CHRISTIAN/INSPIRATIONAL NONFICTION BOOKS FOR YOUNG ADULTS

Growing Up in the Foster Care System – Christian Edition

CHRISTIAN AND INSPIRATIONAL FICTION BOOKS FOR CHILDREN
Hood Christian Picture Book Series for Children

Goodnight, I Wish You Goodnight – Christian Edition – Book 1
Angels, Angels Way Up High, Christian Edition – Book 2
Petting Farm Fun, Christian Edition – Book 3

<u>Upper Middle-Grade Readers – Christian-Themed</u>
<u>Hood Horse Story Series – Christian Edition</u>

Lost Medal – Book 1 – Christian Edition
Saving Sunny – Book 2 – Christian Edition

<u>CHRISTIAN/ INSPIRATIONAL NONFICTION BOOKS FOR CHILDREN</u>

Prayers for Foster Children

The above books are also available in bilingual versions. Please contact Whispering Pine Press International, Inc. for details.
Please note that some books are future books and are currently in production. Please contact us for availability date. Prices are subject to change without notice.
The above list of books is not all-inclusive. For a complete list please visit our website or contact us at:

Whispering Pine Press International, Inc.
P. O. Box 214
Spokane Valley, WA 99037-0214 USA
Phone: (509) 928-6038 | Fax: (509) 922-9949
Email: sales@whisperingpinepress.com
Websites: www.WhisperingPinePress.com
www.WhisperingPinePressBookstore.com
Blog: www.WhisperingPinePressBlog.com

<u>Publisher Websites:</u>

<u>Main Website:</u> WhisperingPinePress.com
<u>Online Store:</u> WhisperingPinePressBookstore.com
<u>WordPress Blogs:</u> WhisperingPinePressBlog.com
WhisperingPinePressKidsBooks.com
WhisperingPinePressTeenBooks.com
WhisperingPinePressPoetry.com

Karen Jean Matsko Hood

Author Website: KarenJeanMatskoHood.com
Online Store: KarenJeanMatskoHoodBookstore.com
Author Blog: KarenJeanMatskoHoodBlog.com
Kids Books: KarensKidsBooks.com
Teen Books: KarensTeenBooks.com

Author's Social Media

Friend her on **Facebook**: Karen Jean Matsko Hood Author Fan Page
Please Follow the Author on **Twitter**: @KarenJeanHood
Google Plus Profile: Karen Jean Matsko Hood
Pinterest.com/KarenJMHood
Linkedin: http://www.linkedin.com/in/KarenJeanMatskoHood
YouTube: http://www.youtube.com/KarenJeanMatskoHood
Instagram: http://instagram.com/KarenJeanMatskoHood
MySpace: https://myspace.com/KarenJeanMatskoHood

Morning Reflections

A Collection of Bible Verses, Prayers, and
Inspirational Poetry for Daily Reflection
Hood Inspirational Reflection Series – Book 1

Karen Jean Matsko Hood

Published by:

Whispering Pine Press International, Inc.
Your Northwest Book Publishing Company

P.O. Box 214
Spokane Valley, WA 99037-0214 USA
Phone: (509) 928-6038 | Fax: (509) 922-9949
Email: sales@whisperingpinepress.com
Websites: www.WhisperingPinePress.com
www.WhisperingPinePressBookstore.com
Blog: www.WhisperingPinePressBlog.com
SAN 253-200X
Printed in the U.S.A.

Published by Whispering Pine Press International, Inc.
P. O. Box 214
Spokane Valley, Washington 99037-0214 USA

Scripture taken from the HOLY BIBLE, NEW INTERNATIONAL VERSION.® Copyright © 1973, 1978, 1984 International Bible Society. Used by permission of Zondervan Publishing House.

For sales outside the United States, please contact the Whispering Pine Press International, Inc., International Sales Department.

Book and Cover Design by Artistic Design Service, Inc.
P.O. Box 1782
Spokane Valley, WA 99037-1782 USA
www.artisticdesignservice.com

Library of Congress Control Number (LCCN): 2014901437

Hood, Karen Jean Matsko
    Title: Morning Reflections: A Collection of Bible Verses, Prayers, and Inspirational Poetry for Daily Reflection

ISBN: 978-0-96793-684-0   case bound
ISBN: 978-1-93094-855-6   perfect bound
ISBN: 978-1-59210-929-6   large print edition
ISBN: 978-1-59210-158-0   audio compact disc
ISBN: 978-1-59808-661-4   audio recording downloadable
ISBN: 978-1-59210-003-3   E-PDF
ISBN: 978-1-59210-914-2   E-PUB
ISBN: 978-1-59434-865-5   E-PRC
ISBN: 978-1-930948-38-9   Whispersync

First Edition: April 2014
1. Prayers, Bible Verses (Morning Reflections: A Collection of Bible Verses, Prayers, and Inspirational Poetry for Daily Reflection) 1. Title

Gift Inscription

To: _____

From: _____

Date: _____

Special Occasion: _____

Special Message: _____

_____

_____

_____

_____

_____

_____

_____

_____

*It is always nice to receive a personal note to
create a special memory.*

Dedications

To my husband and best friend, Jim.

To our seventeen children: Gabriel, Brianne Kristina and her husband Moulik Vinodkumar Kothari, Marissa Kimberly and her husband Kevin Matthew Franck, Janelle Karina and her husband Paul Joseph Turcotte, Mikayla Karlene, Kyler James, Kelsey Katrina, Corbin Joel, Caleb Jerome, Keisha Kalani Hiwot, Devontay Joshua, Kianna Karielle Selam, Rosy Kiara, Mercedes Katherine, Jasmine Khalia Wengel, Cheyenne Krystal, and Annalise Kaylee Marie.

To our grandchild Nola Paige, and future grandchildren.

To our foster grandchildren: Courtney, Lorenzo, and Leah.

To my brother, Stephen, and his wife, Karen.

To my husband's ten siblings: Gary, Colleen, John, Dan, Mary, Ray, Ann, Teresa, Barbara, Agnes, and their families.

In loving memory of my mom, who passed away in 2007; my dad, who passed away in 1976; and my sister, Sandy, who passed away due to multiple sclerosis in 1999.

To Sandy's three sons: Monte, Bradley, and Derek. To Monte's wife, Sarah, and their children: Liam, Alice, Charlie, and Samuel and their foster children. To Bradley's wife, Shawnda, and their children: Anton, Isaac, and Isabel.

To our foster children past and present: Krystal, Sara, Rebecca, Janice, Devontay Joshua, Mercedes Katherine, Zha'Nell, Makia, Onna, Cheyenne Krystal, Onna Marie, Nevaeh, and Zada, our future foster children, and all foster children everywhere.

To the Court Appointed Special Advocate (CASA) Volunteer Program in the judicial system which benefits abused and neglected children.

To the Literacy Campaign dedicated to promoting literacy throughout the world.

Acknowledgements

The author would like to acknowledge all those individuals who helped me during my time in writing this book. Appreciation is extended for all their support and effort they put into this project.

Deep gratitude and profound thanks are owed to my husband, Jim, for giving freely of his time and encouragement during this project.

Thanks are also owed to my children Gabriel, Brianne Kristina and her husband Moulik Vinodkumar Kothari, Marissa Kimberly and her husband Kevin Matthew Franck, Janelle Karina and her husband Paul Joseph Turcotte, Mikayla Karlene, Kyler James, Kelsey Katrina, Corbin Joel, Caleb Jerome, Keisha Kalani Hiwot, Devontay Joshua, Kianna Karielle Selam, Rosy Kiara, Mercedes Katherine, Jasmine Khalia Wengel, Cheyenne Krystal, and Annalise Kaylee Marie. All of these persons inspired my writing.

Thanks are due to Sharron Thompson and Pam Alexandrovich for their assistance in editing and typing this manuscript for publication. Thanks go to Artistic Design Service, Inc. for their assistance in formatting and providing a graphic design of this manuscript for publication. Thank you to Mary Scripture-Smith for designing the pages and the cover.

Thanks also to the three poets Jonathan Johnson, Marvin Bell, and Doreen Gandy Wiley. Encouragement from their seminars and workshops at Lost Horse Press and Pacific Northwest Writers Seminars gave me the confidence to begin and continue writing poems.

Also, a special thanks to my husband Jim for all the work in arranging the poems and shapes here. I could not have completed this book without him.

A great many thanks are due to my family, who were very supportive during the time it took to complete this project. Your patience and support are much appreciated.

Psalm 121

A song of ascents.

¹ I lift up my eyes to the hills—
  where does my help come from?
² My help comes from the LORD,
  the Maker of heaven and earth.

³ He will not let your foot slip—
  he who watches over you will not slumber;
⁴ indeed, he who watches over Israel
  will neither slumber nor sleep.

⁵ The LORD watches over you—
  the LORD is your shade at your right hand;
⁶ the sun will not harm you by day,
  nor the moon by night.

⁷ The LORD will keep you from all harm—
  he will watch over your life;
⁸ the LORD will watch over your coming and going
  both now and forevermore.

Morning Reflections

Table of Contents

Introduction and Invitation

The goal of this book is to invite the reader to reflect upon a collection of Bible verses, related inspirational poetry, and morning prayers related to the Scripture verse. The reader is encouraged to devote some quiet time each morning and use this guide as a morning reflection for your own prayers and spiritual thought throughout the day.

Each page begins with a quote from Scripture followed by a short inspirational poem related to that particular Bible verse. It is followed up with a brief prayer to reflect on the theme of the Scripture passage and the theme of the poem.

We are all busy in our fast-paced, hectic lives. It is important to train ourselves to slow down, pause, and to reflect for a few moments each morning. Try it and I believe you will be pleased with the results in positive attitude throughout the day.

It is my hope that you will take time to appreciate the true joy and beauty given to us each morning and the time to connect and appreciate these moments. I invite you to go forward and add your own prayers and Scripture readings as you wish to enhance and evolve your own "morning reflection."

Remember, life is far too short for all of us. Do pause and reflect for a few moments each morning. Combine this reflection with prayer, and encourage your loved ones to do the same.

Take care and enjoy your own personal morning reflection, devotion, and prayers. May God bless all of us!

Karen Jean Matsko Hood

Prayer of Francis of Assisi

Lord, make me a
    channel of thy peace.

Where there is hatred, let me sow love;
Where there is injury, pardon;
Where there is doubt, faith;
Where there is despair, hope;
Where there is darkness, light;
Where there is sadness, joy.

O Divine Master
Grant that I may not so much seek
to be consoled, as to console;
to be understood, as to understand;
to be loved, as to love.
For it is in giving that we receive;
it is in pardoning that we are pardoned;
it is in dying that we are born into Eternal Life.

Amen

    Francis of Assisi

Rejoice in God

Do not be anxious about anything, but in everything, by prayer and petition, with thanksgiving, present your requests to God. And the peace of God, which transcends all understanding, will guard your hearts and your minds in Christ Jesus.

Philippians 4:6-7

Rejoice in God

There are times when all seems gloomy,
dark, and lifeless.
Tension and stress smother as
I fret and worry.
I feast on stress again,
then a robin of spring arrives
and knocks at my door;
a season to pray and ask for help,
to release my fear to joy.
Rejoice in God ... I say again, rejoice.
It is time to reflect on joy and beauty,
to thank God for all the good.
Yes, it is time to say
rejoice in God ... I say again, rejoice!

Dear God,

Help me to be joyful today, no matter what my circumstances. It is easy to focus on unpleasant events in my daily life: tension, struggle, decision, challenge, criticism, or conflict. The Apostle Paul wrote the above passage while in prison. If Paul can find a way to be joyful while oppressed in prison, then I can find a way to rejoice in my own life, my journey. Help me to find balance, wholeness, truth, an integral life. Amen.

All Day

Let your face shine on your servant; save me in your unfailing love.

Psalm 31:16

All Day

Morning mist hangs
like a cotton canopy,
freely afloat in the wind.

Surrealistic magic carpets
lay under rays of morning sun.
Miraculous surroundings
remind me
that I am not alone.

A higher power of goodness
designs this haze of mystery.
Help me trust in You.
Have mercy on me.
I trust in You
all day,
every day.

Dear Lord,

Some mornings I awaken, still half asleep, and walk a prayerful pilgrimage of reflection in my mind. I imagine the most beautiful mist enlightening the landscape. I feel Your warmth shining down on me from above, piercing through the mist, warming me and leading me closer to You, the ultimate servant leader.

Your unfailing love reaches me despite my imperfections. Please forgive me for my poor choices, and help me trust in You as my servant leader. Amen.

Call on the Name of the Lord

Everyone who calls on the name of the Lord will be saved.

Romans 10:13

Call on the Name of the Lord

It sounds so easy
to call Your name.
To be saved with a name.

Yet, the name does not always
reach our soul, or
our mind.

Call out to the Lord.
Make sure Your voice drenches
our spirit, cleanses our mind.
As we call out,
we sing for salvation.

Please help all who live
call on the name of the Lord.
We pray to be saved this morning
and every day.

Dear Lord,

Please help all who live call on the name of the Lord. I pray to be saved this morning and every day. Please help me to pray each day and to trust Your guidance. Help me to live out Your name and everything it represents. God, I ask for Your forgiveness by repenting my sins. I freely submit myself to You on this day and every day after. This morning I pray that everyone who lives will call out Your name today. Help me to live Your Word this morning and every morning. Amen.

Message to God's Beloved Son

As soon as Jesus was baptized, he went up out of the water. At that moment heaven was opened, and he saw the Spirit of God descending like a dove and lighting on him. And a voice from heaven said, "This is my Son, whom I love; with him I am well pleased."

Matthew 3:16-17

Message To God's Beloved Son

Great is the gift this morning.
The gift of Your Son, Jesus Christ.
Love is a gift to hold in our hearts,
an instrument that warms the soul.

Keep our hearts alive,
rekindle our love,
our passion for life,
our respect for others.
Help us share our gifts from God.

Help us listen to
the butterflies that walk on tiptoes,
to hear Your message,
and send our reply.

I listen to the stillness.
Dear God,
help us follow Your voice
today and always.

Dear Jesus,

Your passion continues to inspire throughout the ages. Your sacrifice is the ultimate sign of unconditional love. Please help me to better walk with You, and help me model Your hospitality and unlimited love, to better merit Your sacrifice. Help me to become a loyal follower. Amen.

Morning Beam

By the word of the Lord were the heavens made, their starry host by the breath of his mouth.

Psalm 33:6

Morning Beam

I sit at my writing table and
look at the sunbeam,
bright, and illuminating as it dances from
one windowpane to another.

Such innocence, pure,
so simple and calm.
Sunbeams play with the
wildflowers that move.

Distant meadows
frame mountains and
punctuate pine trees
dressed in long needles.

Soothing sunbeams,
stay this morning,
my celebration, my
morning bliss.

Dear Lord,

Thank You Lord for such majesty. Thank You for the morning sunbeams, the gift You send us to enjoy. Every time I see a sunbeam from the starry heavens, help me to remember that I should say a prayer of thanksgiving to You. Thank You for Your breath of creation. Thank You for the gift of life. Amen.

Clap Your Hands

Clap your hands, all you nations; shout to God with cries of joy.

Psalm 47:1

Clap Your Hands

Tick, tock, clap, rejoice.
Tick, tock, sing, rejoice.
Tick, tock, shout, and sing.

Rejoice with your voice
to hear God's music.
Clap your hands and praise

your God with your song.
God has given you a voice
and hands.

Use them to sing and
praise your God.

Clap your hands with songs
of joy. Give praise to God.

Dear God,

This morning I will sing to You with bliss, shout Your honor, and harmonize my hands. St. Benedict, known for his wisdom, sanctity, and miracles, believed that when one sings, he or she prays twice. O Lord, help me to sing out today and give You praise. I love You and shall sing Your praises. Help me to sing always to You, Lord, this morning and every day. Amen.

Vulnerable Lamb

The LORD is the strength of his people, a fortress of salvation for his anointed one. Save your people and bless your inheritance; be their shepherd and carry them forever.

Psalm 28:8-9

Vulnerable Lamb

I am a fuzzy lamb,
warm and vulnerable,
in need of protection,
looking for a shepherd kind.

It is You, Lord, with Your love,
gentle shepherd.
You can keep me under Your watch
forever, O Lord.

Be my shepherd;
I am Your love.

I am Your
vulnerable lamb.

Dear God,

I pray to You and ask You for salvation. Please transform my life in every aspect. I want to surrender my life to Your ideal plan. Protect me and guide me as a shepherd. Thank You for the freedom to choose to follow Your way.

Help me show the transforming power of Your salvation to my family and my loved ones through the example of my life. Help me live my faith as an example of Your mercy and love. This I ask of You, O Lord. Amen.

Daily Rejoice

Finally, brothers, good-bye. Aim for perfection, listen to my appeal, be of one mind, live in peace. And the God of love and peace will be with you.
2 Corinthians 13:11

Daily Rejoice

Looking out my kitchen window,
I see the moonlit sun that
rises in beauty over peaceful meadows.
Dew droplets glisten on blades of grass as
swirls of wind awaken flowers that sleep.
Off in the distance a tree frog sings
while crickets drift to sleep, to
rejoice in the simple pleasures.
Creation was given
as a gift from God.
I listen to the song of birds,
the babble of water, as we try to
live in peace with one another and
rejoice in the God of love.

Dear God,

This morning please help me reflect on my need to amend my ways. Lord, teach me to always aim for precision and peace. Help me to make harmony by learning to focus on others instead of myself. Please help me to become a good role model for others so that they may rejoice and share in Your loving peace. Amen.

Water Walk

When the disciples saw him walking on the lake, they were terrified. "It's a ghost," they said, and cried out in fear. But Jesus immediately said to them: "Take courage! It is I. Don't be afraid."

Matthew 14:26-27

Water Walk

Followers of the Holy One look out at still water.
Quiet waters are present some days.
Mostly I encounter rough waves
and cannot calm the storm that is
exploding beneath thin surface.

Followers watch and cannot explain.
Help me, Lord, build my faith.
Help me read Your Word
and live Your example.
Oh, Lord, we pray to You
this morning.
Help me live in quiet waters,
and pray always for waters still.

Dear Lord,

Thank You for the moments of quiet waters, reflection time. Lord, I thank You for the moments when the waters are rough. I thank You when You hold out Your hand and tell me, "Take courage; don't be afraid." It is only You who can take control of the rough waters in my life and cause them to be still. I praise You for the peace You give me. Help me live in courage so that I may walk and choose the correct path to You. Amen.

Light of the World

When Jesus spoke again to the people, he said, "I am the light of the world. Whoever follows me will never walk in darkness, but will have the light of life."

John 8:12

Light of the World

Mystery surrounds reason.
Bright rays of sun pierce through the canopy of darkness.
The arrival of dawn begins;
one tree, then another,
begins to shimmer with iridescent reflections.
Tiny droplets of scattered dew shine and disappear in evaporation.

Rays of sunshine
give my eyes the light to see
to walk out of darkness
and know the true light of the world.

Dear Lord,

I praise You for being my light in the darkness. Your light brings hope to me. I pray that I can follow Your beacon of light. Jesus, Your perfect example shines bright against this world. By Your example, as recorded in the Gospels, I cannot hide in sinful ignorance, but must follow in Your light. I pray for the strength to follow in Your footsteps and for the courage to reflect Your light through my life. Dear Lord, thank You for being the saving light of the world. Amen.

Morning Path

John replied in the words of Isaiah the prophet, "I am the voice of one calling in the desert, 'Make straight the way for the Lord.'"

John 1:23

Morning Path

Parched sands thirst for moisture.
Tears stream down tired cheeks,
sullen, worn and desperate souls,
alone in the desert.

Morning brings new light
to illuminate our paths.
Different walkways in desert sand
help me see the correct path
in this morning light.

Dear Lord,

Sometimes I am in pain and feel isolated in a dry desert that parches my soul. During this time of pain and feeling alone in the desert, help me to remember that I must follow Your path. Today, I pray that I make the right choices throughout the day. Help me use this morning to plan my day to live in goodness. For this I pray, dear Lord. Amen.

Great Things

All of them were filled with the Holy Spirit and began to speak in other tongues as the Spirit enabled them.

Acts 2:4

Great Things

Holy Spirit, You elude me.
It is You I try to put my arms around.
I yearn to hug You, to talk to You.
It is my wish to ask You questions of wisdom,
thoughtful questions that You would answer.

Instead, my role is to find Your spirit
within my heart. Not a hug or a handshake,
but a beating heart You give me. A
clear mind You give me in a gift-wrapped
package for me alone to open.

Dear Holy Spirit,

Elusive Holy Spirit, remind me to pray to You and seek You out. I need You. I love You. I praise You, Holy Spirit. I am not worthy of this sacred gift of love. Help me accept this love and share it with others. I pray to You, Holy Spirit, that I may carry Your whisper of wisdom within me and share it with others. Amen.

Expectation

Lamentations 3:25

Expectation

White clouds stream above my head,
beyond my touch.
I look up and wonder
about the meaning of life.

What should I see?
What do I search for past the clouds?
Beyond my touch?
Beyond my leap?

Why do some hope each day,
to touch the skies and
know Your love, Your presence?
Why do others despair each day?
Others mourn in gray storm clouds that
block the sun of light overhead.

Realize that dull haze above brings
fresh spring rain to nurture our crops,
that feed our souls in expectation.

Dear God,

On this morning, I offer up my devotion to You. Help me share my wish, that all lives can be touched by You. I have hope that all people can learn to have faith and peace in You. I search for Your love and put my lively, tenacious hope and trust in You. I hope and pray that all will seek You. Amen.

Spring Morning

*The L*ORD *is in his holy temple; the L*ORD *is on his heavenly throne. He observes the sons of men; his eyes examine them.*

Psalm 11:4

Spring Morning

Good morning, Lord. What joy You bring, dear God.
The robins hop on swirls of grass.
Daffodils burst from buttercup buds,
crabapple blossoms unfold pink beauty.

Thank You, God, for this spring day.
Your bounty in nature is beautiful,
tributes for us to enjoy.
Thanks, dear Lord, for Your creation.
Help me recognize Your awesome handiwork.
Help me share Your mercy
and generosity with people in need.

Dear Lord,

Sometimes I forget to appreciate the beauty You have created around me. Thank You for pink blossoms, the robins, and the yellow daffodils. Thank You for painting this beautiful morning canvas around me. Help me to truly see the beauty of Your creation. Amen.

Bees of Life

Rejoice in the LORD, you who are righteous, and praise his holy name.
Psalm 97:12

Bees of Life

I saw a bee on a tree.
Thank You, God.
I could eat honey from the bee
that You made. Thank You, God.
That yellow bee made my drink sweet with
honey, in this morning tea ...
all because You made the flowers.
Beautiful flower petals
decorated with luscious pollen.
Help me appreciate the small, the bees,
the lowly, the workers.
Help me respect all nature, all
workers under the sun.
Thank You, Lord. Alleluia.

Dear God,

Thank You for the glorious morning. Thank You, God, in full grandeur. Guide me to live in Your kingdom and make my place Yours. I pray to You, God, that I may be worthy of Your love. I offer thanks to You this morning. Help me rejoice in my daily work in my community. Please help me so that I may serve others and live as a good example as I rejoice in Your name. Amen.

Our Father

"This, then, is how you should pray: " 'Our Father in heaven, hallowed be your name, your kingdom come, your will be done on earth as it is in heaven. Give us today our daily bread. Forgive us our debts, as we also have forgiven our debtors. And lead us not into temptation, but deliver us from the evil one.' "

Matthew 6:9-13

Our Father

Our Father.
How great You are.
Thank You, Father, for this great morning.
I see the beauty of Your creation.
Help me see the beauty of Your
gift of life in every soul around me.
Sometimes it is not so easy
for me to understand.
Sometimes it is not so easy
for me to live.
Help me, Lord, Amen.

Dear Lord,

This morning I pray the wonderful prayer of "Our Father." Today I promise to pray this prayer from my heart many times. By repeating this prayer, I know that I am reciting this prayer the way Jesus would want me to pray. Deliver me from evil, oh Lord. To You I pray today and every day. Amen.

Shepherd

The LORD is my shepherd, I shall not be in want. He makes me lie down in green pastures, he leads me beside quiet waters, he restores my soul. He guides me in paths of righteousness for his name's sake. Even though I walk through the valley of the shadow of death, I will fear no evil, for you are with me; your rod and your staff, they comfort me.

Psalm 23:1-4

Shepherd

Shepherds watch their flocks;
they feed them and keep them safe.

They guide them from troubled waters,
move them to abundant grasses.

Make sure we have ample grains
and sweet water of life.

Cleanse us from evil and make
sure we stand in the light.

God is our strength;
shepherd us to safety.

Dear God,

This morning I stand on green grass and drink sweet water. I pray that You will shepherd me and keep me as a safe lamb in Your flock. I love You, Lord. Help me serve as an example of the way in which You would like us to live. Help me live a good life. For this I pray to You, Lord God. Amen.

Good Morning

*The L*ORD *your God will raise up for you a prophet like me from among your own brothers. You must listen to him.*

Deuteronomy 18:15

Good Morning

Good morning, God.
Help me follow Your prophecy
today and all days.
Help me reflect on Your Bible verse.

Help me listen to Your message, and
remind me to read from the Bible.
Let me hear what it is You say to me.
These are my needs upon which to reflect.
Help me listen to Your prophets this morning,
and all mornings.

Dear God,

Please help me remember to listen to Your message and lead the life You want me to live. Help me remember to follow in Your path each day, not blindly but with reverence and reason, to remember that I am here for a purpose. Help me each morning to live out Your just cause in my life. Amen.

The Lord is My Shepherd

"I am the good shepherd; I know my sheep and my sheep know me."
John 10:14

The Lord is My Shepherd

A shepherd is a caretaker of animals
soft and needing protection.
Shepherds watch over their flock
with kindness and care.

Help me become a good shepherd
of those around me.
Help me give myself to others.

Dear Lord,

Thank You for being the good shepherd. Thank You, Jesus, for watching over me this morning and for recognizing me as one of Your sheep. I pray this morning for loyalty in following Your army of protection. You guide me from dangers and lead the way to righteousness. I pray that I can be faithful in following You, my good shepherd. Thank You, Lord, for Your continuous compassion and infinite mercy. Help me also to shepherd kindly each of Your creations. Amen.

Forgiveness

Bear with each other and forgive whatever grievances you may have against one another. Forgive as the Lord forgave you.

Colossians 3:13

Forgiveness

Forgiveness, such a trying task,
perhaps the most difficult of all.

Jesus Christ was loving and kind,
always ready to forgive
beyond the scope of time.

It is baffling
to forgive those who cause pain.
Harder still, to forgive our enemies.

I lift my eyes
and say I forgive.

It is so necessary for me.
Help me once again
to learn this demanding task,
to forgive all others.

Forgive each and every day,
this morning and all the mornings of my life.

Dear Jesus,

Help me to reflect upon Your kindness and Your ability to forgive. Please grant me the ability to forgive others as You have so honorably taught. It is easy to forgive those who have been kind to me, but I ask for help to remember to be kind to those who are unkind to me. Amen.

Help Me, Lord

O Lord, do not forsake me; be not far from me, O my God. Come quickly to help me, O Lord my Savior.

Psalm 38:21-22

Help Me, Lord

Walking down the curved path down the hill,
I look up and see the trees towering to the sky,
reaching upward toward some life I do not
understand.

Together we work. We toil, we wonder.
Forgive me for worrying so much about life,
about You.
Help me nourish deep faith. I yearn to know You
deep within my soul.

I need to know You will not abandon me.
I simply do not know Your plan.
My plan may not be Your plan. I love You, Lord.

Dear Lord,

This morning, I wake up and feel afraid. I ask that You hear me in seeking Your guidance today. I explore the path that I've detoured from in the past. I ask for Your comfort and guidance during these days that lay ahead. Help me to feel Your strength within me and to heed Your will and not count the cost. Amen.

Morning Faith

"If that is how God clothes the grass of the field, which is here today and tomorrow is thrown into the fire, will he not much more clothe you, O you of little faith?"

Matthew 6:30

Morning Faith

Field of grass,
Lord of creation,
help me find the message,
the journey to follow
through my life.
This morning I pray
for deeper faith.
Help me, God, to
grow in Your love
and mercy.
Help me grow
in faith with
each blossom that appears.

Dear Lord,

Thank You for the sunrise and the fields of pasture and flowers. Sometimes I do not understand the events of the day and am worried. Today, help me become a better person and to have total faith in You, my Lord. Let me continue to walk along the path of my life with faith toward truth, reverence, and universal love. Amen.

The Well

When a Samaritan woman came to draw water, Jesus said to her, "Will you give me a drink?" (His disciples had gone into the town to buy food). The Samaritan woman said to him, "You are a Jew and I am a Samaritan woman. How can you ask me for a drink?" (For Jews do not associate with Samaritans). Jesus answered her, "If you knew the gift of God and who it is that asks you for a drink, you would have asked him and he would have given you living water."

John 4:7-10

The Well

Men and women created equal,
equal in the eyes of God.
Then society emerges
and decides on who has the power.
The authority they gave to men.
Patriarchal society
we did become
with men in charge of all,
women in charge of none.
Now it is time
for women to be heard,
to be treated with fairness
as Jesus treated women.
He listened to
the woman at the well.

Dear Jesus,

Thank You for Your kindness and Your gentleness toward women. This morning remind me to do the same and serve as a fine example of Your treatment of all women as the woman at the well. Please help all people of the world learn to respect women. Help all cultures love and show kindness to all women. Amen.

44

Glorious Praise

*Shout for joy to the L*ORD*, all the earth, burst into jubilant song with music; make music to the L*ORD *with the harp, with the harp and the sound of singing, with trumpets and the blast of the ram's horn—shout for joy before the L*ORD*, the King. Let the sea resound, and everything in it, the world, and all who live in it.*

Psalm 98:4-7

Glorious Praise

Glorious praise in inner spirit,
praise God in all of God's almighty wonder.
Look out my morning window.
I am in awe at this magnificent creation.

Nature abounds in mysterious beauty.
Tall towering Ponderosa pines sing
to gleeful tree frogs next to black crickets.
All songs of praise are gifts of the wind.

Let the earth sing out to God.
Let us praise God each morning.
Let us pray for God's Glory.
Halleluiah!

Dear God,

Help me focus on the wonders of Your glorious creation and praise the glory of Your name. Thank You for the height of the mountains and the wonder of the hummingbird. I praise You today for all creation. I pray to You today and every day. Amen.

Morning Arrival

And do this, understanding the present time. The hour has come for you to wake up from your slumber, because our salvation is nearer now than when we first believed.

Romans 13:11

Morning Arrival

Morning arrives with sunrays that
knock on the pane of glass to
call me amidst its radiant light.

Help me grow in Your radiance,
to awaken from my sleep,
to be alert and kind,
to follow Your goodness,
and be simply aware
of Your bountiful creation
in Your gift of morning light.

Dear God,

Help me remember this morning to awaken clearly from my sleep. Help me to be alert and empathetic to everyone around me. Help me feel other people's happiness and to better understand their sorrow. Please help me follow Your path this day so that I, too, can have an experience of consciousness and know my purpose here on earth. Amen.

Help for the Poor

"If one of your countrymen becomes poor and is unable to support himself among you, help him as you would an alien or temporary resident, so he can continue to live among you."

Leviticus 25:35

Help for the Poor

Good morning, Lord.
This morning I ask You to encourage me
with Your graces, gentleness, and goodness,
to help the poor.

This morning, help me to remember the poor,
the suffering, and the sick.
Today, help me to give myself
vigorously to the poor.

In some minute way,
I will help the poor.
This morning, I promise to give some
clothes and food.
Today, for this I pray.

Dear God,

This morning, please help me remember that I should aid the poor. Very often, I am negligent and forget to think about other people. Today, help me to develop a plan that will help the marginal members of society. The poor abound in different ways. Help me find my own personal way to create a difference in this world. Also, instead of waiting until I discover a grand plan, help me to offer what I have to the less fortunate now. I promise I will help, and it is up to me to create the opportunity. Amen.

Song of Delight

Sing to the LORD a new song, for he has done marvelous things; his right hand and his holy arm have worked salvation for him.

Psalm 98:1

Song of Delight

Meadowlark melodies capture my ear
as chickadees chatter on pine trees,
with songs of delight.

Babies babble and gently coo
as little children chuckle,
a chorus of delight.

Help me share and pass the song,
the melody my neighbor sings,
a chorus of delight.

Dear Lord,

I pray to You this morning in song. I thank You for Your marvelous deeds. Help me remember to share my life with others. Lord, help me to recognize the opportunities you provide to share a special gift with a friend, so they may sing praise to You. Amen.

Savior

"I, even I, am the Lord, and apart from me there is no savior. I have revealed and saved and proclaimed—I, and not some foreign god among you. You are my witnesses," declares the Lord, "that I am God."

Isaiah 43:11-12

Savior

What does it mean to believe in our Savior?
Excuse me, Lord, because
I do not always know
the steps or the reason.
Oh, dear Lord, I ask
You now. I ask You for help
to follow the road.
Help me to understand
Your suffering, my Savior.
I love You, God, and wait
to tell You how much I thank
You for being my Savior.
I love You today and all days, my Lord,
my Savior.
Thank You for Your creation and our salvation.
Amen.

Dear Lord,

I praise You this morning for being my Savior. Thank You for revealing Yourself to me; You are the one true God. Lord, use me as Your witness to show others that You are God. Use me to show those around me that only through You is there hope of salvation. Amen.

Heal the Lowly

The Spirit of the sovereign LORD is on me, because the LORD has anointed me to preach good news to the poor. He has sent me to bind up the brokenhearted, to proclaim freedom for the captives and release from darkness for the prisoners.

Isaiah 61:1

Heal the Lowly

Heal the lowly—what a message.
For I am lowly, the lowest of the low.
Help me to remember my pain.
Pin it close to my heart.
Help me reach out to others,
to let them know that
they are not alone.
Help me to offer myself,
to give to the lowly.
Help me reach out
to heal the heartbroken
split because of pain.
Accept the ointment.
Sing glad tidings of joy.

Dear Lord,

Thank You for reminding me to preach good news to the lowly and to help heal the brokenhearted. Sometimes in my busy life, I forget to help those around me. This morning, help me to think of people in my life that are depressed and brokenhearted. Help me think of ways to bring Your message to them and create a generous heart. I pray that I have the courage and compassion today to carry out kind acts to others. Amen.

Shout to God

Shout with joy to God, all the earth! Sing the glory of his name; make his praise glorious!

Psalm 66:1-2

Shout to God

I am shy and do not want to shout,
but then I marvel at the wonder
of creation and shout with energy.
For God can hear us shout for joy ...
even if it is a whisper.

We should clap our hands,
sing with joy,
praise the Lord.

We shout and sing
with gladness, and
give praise to the Lord.
Sing the glory of His name.
Make His praise glorious.

Dear Lord,

I know how wonderful You are, and I praise You for this wonderful morning. Thank You, God, for everything You have done. I love You Lord; I love You this morning and always. I trust in You, God, through prayer. Dear Lord, please help me this morning and every morning to begin my day with prayer and then to live the rest of the day in prayer. Amen.

Blessed

And he passed in front of Moses, proclaiming, "The Lord, the Lord, the compassionate and gracious God, slow to anger, abounding in love and faithfulness, maintaining love to thousands, and forgiving wickedness, rebellion and sin."

Exodus 34:6-7a

Blessed

Blessed be God, for He is our only God.
Blessed be God's Son, Jesus, so enlightening.

Blessed be the Holy Spirit.
Blessed be my inner soul and strength.

Blessed be God, the Holy One.
Blessed be God, the Creator.

Blessed be the light
that brightens my path.

Please lead me down
the trail of the disquieting,

so that I may spread the message of
love to each soul in the blessed village.

Dear Lord,

Blessed be You, the Creator, and blessed be Your only Son. Oh, cherished God, I love You and am not worthy of all Your blessings. You are compassionate and gracious, abounding in love. Please forgive my upheavals and sins. Please help and bless me on this morning and every morning here and after. Amen.

God's Glory

"And the glory of the Lord will be revealed, and all mankind together will see it. For the mouth of the LORD has spoken."

Isaiah 40:5

God's Glory

Morning brings glory of dawn's new day.
Help me remember this in every way.

Glory of God today is revealed.
My love for God unfolds each day.

Help me love every woman and man.
Remind me to complete kind deeds today
in an affectionate way.

Help me in everything I say.
This morning, dear Lord, I pray.

Dear Lord,

Help me to be joyful and remember Your glory on this morning. Help me and all mankind realize Your saving power. I offer my morning, my day, and my month to You. Help me to see Your glory in all things. Amen.

Morning Walk

I will sing to the LORD all my life; I will sing praise to my God as long as I live. May my meditation be pleasing to him, as I rejoice in the LORD.
                                                            Psalm 104:33-34

Morning Walk

I walk along the noisy path
to see a beautiful butterfly blue.
Vibrant colors and patterns of every palette color.
What a moment
to enjoy.
A minute to rejoice.
Yellow, gold, and
painted spots.
Patina shimmers to
liven the morning canvas.
I walk and meditate
this beautiful morning
that God has given me.

Dear Lord,

Help me to rejoice and to be happy with this beautiful morning. I am going to take a few minutes to be quiet and praise You for all the things for which I am grateful. Thank You for Your kindness, and help me to be kind to all whom I encounter today. Help me to be happy and to rejoice, for I know You are near. I pray that this joy will remain and be modeled all day. Amen.

Be Not Afraid

They cried out, because they all saw him and were terrified. Immediately he spoke to them and said, "Take courage! It is I. Don't be afraid."

Mark 6: 49b-50

Be Not Afraid

Be not afraid.
These are three easy words.
Yet, I am afraid
of the night and beyond,
of the evil I see … and worse.
The evil dresses in pleasing clothing.
Why is there evil out there
in disguise, not exposed?
Help me to recognize both good and evil.
Help me recognize evil
that is hidden.
Fear opposes hope.
Give me fortitude.
Help me, Lord.
Help me be not afraid.

Dear Lord,

I pray to You this morning for courage and strength. I am afraid of the unknown, fearful of the future. I know You are with me and that I should take courage from Your presence. On this morning, I pray for the strength and fortitude to overcome my fears. I take refuge in Your radiance. My hope resides in You. You are light, music, love. Amen.

Mercy

"But love your enemies, do good to them, and lend to them without expecting to get anything back. Then your reward will be great, and you will be sons of the Most High, because he is kind to the ungrateful and wicked. Be merciful, just as your Father is merciful."

Luke 6:35-36

Mercy

We trust in Your mercy, O Lord,
honesty and benevolence,
kindness and tenderness,
charity and humanity are all
gifts we need to
share with one another.
Help us forgive our
enemies this morning
and every morning.
Help me follow Your example
of mercy.

Dear Lord,

Please help me to follow Your laws and Your direction. Bolster me to follow Your example by being merciful to others. Give me the strength to love my enemies, even when I know they might not return the love. Your love for me encourages me to give to people whom I know will not likely be able to repay me. O God, I desire to be Your child and love as You do. Your loving care is a model for how we need to treat one another. Help me to use the gifts of sympathy and compassion that You have given me. Amen.

God's Son

While he was still speaking, a bright cloud enveloped them, and a voice from the cloud said, "This is my Son, whom I love; with him I am well pleased. Listen to him!"

Matthew 17:5

God's Son

Today we think of God's Son.
He is beloved through all ages,

age of past, age of present.
Yes, we also must love His Son.

In the future and each day,
as Christians, we see God's glory.

Good news of Christ, His Son,
reminds us of His grace on the cross.

God tells us to
listen to His Son.

Do listen to Him.

Dear Jesus Christ,

Please help me to remember the message from Your Father today. I know that I am supposed to listen to You and follow Your example. Help me reflect on Your message this morning and to find a way to model Your life until the world's end and thereafter. Amen.

Music in the Wind

Sing praises to the LORD, enthroned in Zion; proclaim among the nations what he has done.

Psalm 9:11

Music in the Wind

Air stirs around me; I hear mysterious sounds.
Low notes resonate with high notes clear.
Treble and bass intertwine.
Harps and tympanis combine.

Such clear notes move my soul,
to save all people in all nations,
through our work, through our prayers.
For peace and love,
to save all humans throughout the world.

For this I pray,
dear God, in music,
to the universe, amen.

Dear Lord,

Thank You for Your beautiful music around me. Thank You for Your majestic voice. This morning, help me to live in honesty so that I can praise in Your beautiful voice. Help me work toward a peaceful, loving life, equanimity. For this I pray this morning. Amen.

Wrapped Packages

He will cover you with his feathers, and under his wings you will find refuge; his faithfulness will be your shield and rampart.

Psalm 91:4

Wrapped Packages

God announces the truth of creation.
Skies so blue display this divine function,
in waters of the oceans and lakes.
Sometimes we forget to thank the Giver.
We sometimes do not see.

Package adorned so perfectly.
Such ideal gift-wrap stretched out far and wide.
Ponderosa pine trees cloaked in their long, deep green,
fragrant and aromatic. Refreshing
tamarack dressed in needles changing with the seasons;

lush green and thick in summer,
disrobed in winter.
Blue, swift skies decorated with
white, fluffy clouds, shift with the gift of wind
while stars twinkle, as eyes sparkle in darkness.

Dear Lord,

Good morning, God. Thank You for Your gifts. Help me find comfort in Your love. I pray that I will be faithful and that my faith will grow in love. Amen.

Children, Our Flowers

But Jesus called the children to him and said, "Let the little children come to me, and do not hinder them, for the kingdom of God belongs to such as these. I tell you the truth, anyone who will not receive the kingdom of God like a little child will never enter it."

Luke 18:16-17

Children, Our Flowers

Children are like flowers.
What a beautiful bouquet they make.
A collection of flowers that dance.
Flowers that need our care
to nourish and cherish each day.
We will protect these flowers
from the approach of weeds.
Give them plenty of bright sunlight,
make sure their roots anchor.
When we care for and love
these flowers,
petals will grow and blossom …
into elegance.
Red flowers, blue flowers, pink flowers
unfold to make a beautiful bouquet,
perfume to please all senses,
music to our ears.
Children are our flowers, a
lovely and treasured bouquet.

Dear Lord,

Thank You for this morning and for all the beautiful children in the world. Help me show kindness and love to each child I meet. The image of a good disciple is a small child. Children are unique and such wonderful gifts from You. Help me to appreciate this morning bouquet. Amen.

Sometimes I Am Lonely

My God, my God, why have you forsaken me? Why are you so far from saving me, so far from the words of my groaning?

Psalm 22:1

Sometimes I Am Lonely

Sometimes I am lonely,
and wake up with sadness in my heart.

Sometimes in my pain I cry out,
and ask why have You abandoned me?

Then I realize I am wrong.
You have not left me; You are always there.
It is my choice to accept You or deny You.

Help me to remember that not only sometimes,
but always You are there for me.

Dear Lord,

Sometimes I am sad, lonely, and even depressed. I need to remind myself that You are always near. Please help me remember You are there for me. Please help me grow in Your love and presence this morning and all through each day. I pray to You today to also help others that are lonely. Help me, help them know You are there. Amen.

Hardened Hearts

Today, if you hear his voice, do not harden your hearts.

Psalm 95:7b-8a

Hardened Hearts

There are hardened hearts around us,
hardened hearts within us.
Yet, we only hear silence.
We need to listen for His voice.
Do you hear
silence or the voice?
Harden not your hearts.
Hear His message
and make your heart
loving and good.
Today we will listen to His voice.

Dear Lord,

Please help me to stay away from hardening hearts. All too often I am guilty of being harsh, judgmental, and unwilling to listen to Your voice. Help me to follow the humanity lived out by Christ. Teach me to ask questions to learn and grow, not judgmental questions. Help me to hear Your voice and follow it. I desire Your will in my life. You challenge me to remove all sinful desires from my spirit, and sometimes negativity is difficult to release, but I know that Your desire for my life is love. O Lord, I offer up my heart to You this morning. Amen.

Sing Praise

Sing to the LORD a new song, for he has done marvelous things; his right hand and his holy arm have worked salvation for him. The Lord has made his salvation known and revealed his righteousness to the nations.

Psalm 98:1-2

Sing Praise

Sing a song of beautiful colors.
Sing a song for every season.
Sing a song of roses,
mixed with smiles of daisies.
Canaries carry the melody
while chickadees chatter
on crackling pines,
all standing in Your glory.
Blades of grass
in chorus with
tall oak tress
sing the song of creation.
The baby coos to
Grandma's song,
as moms and dads
say their prayers.
What marvelous deeds
God has revealed!
Do we stop to see
His beautiful power?

Dear Lord,

Help me to sing a song of prayer today and share it with my family, that they may hear my song. Sometimes, I am so busy that I do not notice all Your wonders of creation. Dear Lord, I praise You this morning; You are so powerful. Grant me awareness, and help me share it. Amen.

Creation Joy

So God made the expanse and separated the water under the expanse from the water above it. And it was so.

Genesis 1:7

Creation Joy

Oh dear God, I run into the wall of beauty,
the shrine of creation, the joy of the world.

My morning tea greets me with warmth,
the fragrant leaves soothe.

Yet, out the window a robin works
across the field in blades of green.

Fragrant peony heads attach to green and
bob in the wind to remind me
that God is good indeed.

Dear Lord,

Please help me this morning to remember the water, the light, life, and the rain of spring. Thank You for the clouds, and the seas, and for the spring flowers, and all the life that is sustained by the waters that You have created. On this hopeful morning, I pray to thank You for the goodness of Your creation that brings beauty to all life. Amen.

Spirit of God

And if the Spirit of him who raised Jesus from the dead is living in you, he who raised Christ from the dead will also give life to your mortal bodies through his Spirit, who lives in you.

Romans 8:11

Spirit of God

I am shy and do not want to shout to You,
Spirit of God. Hidden in mystery,
while movement oscillates, circles
like spokes of the August fan.

That rotating breeze I feel. Clouds move,
I see music of the songbird. I hear You.
Where are You my Spirit?
Know me, O Spirit. Alleluia.

Spirit of God
I love You and praise You.

Dear Lord,

I live to deserve Your love. Please forgive me for my ignorance in understanding. Help me deepen my faith. I love You, God. Let Your Spirit work in my life, and help my faith to grow daily as a spiritually mature human being. Amen.

Narrow Gate

"Enter through the narrow gate. For wide is the gate and broad is the road that leads to destruction, and many enter through it. But small is the gate and narrow the road that leads to life, and only a few find it."

Matthew 7:13-14

Narrow Gate

Upon birth, a choice we are given.
An invasive choice shaped in the form of a path.
The journey down the path does not grant self-immunity,
nor does it conceal us from our darkest fears.
Moreover, it is an undying seed
that leads to the narrow gate of everlasting life.
Embark on this grand journey, and make an honest choice.
A choice set before us from the powers that be,
the power from our Lord and Savior.
The struggle to find the narrow gate is epic,
but the reward is eternal.

Dear Lord,

I praise You for revealing Your narrow road to me and that I might follow it to everlasting life. O Lord, help me stay on the right path throughout every situation I face, no matter how tempting it is to take the easier way out. Help me enter through the narrow gate and not follow others into destruction. Thank You for providing a way, freedom, and mature ethics, that lead to a voyage of discovery. Amen.

Heart Cleansing

"A new command I give you: Love one another. As I have loved you, so you must love one another. By this all men will know that you are my disciples, if you love one another."

John 13:34-35

Heart Cleansing

My heart continues daily
because of You.

You created me in Your goodness.
Help my heart remain loving.

It is up to me
to live in kindness,

to forgive others.
Yet, this is not always easy.

Help me appreciate the white
peony blossom as it unfolds.

Help me notice the children
in need of love.

Help me to live in tranquility.
Help me live in kindness.

Dear Lord,

Day after day, I try to live better in kindness and love. I don't always do a good job of this, but I ask for Your forgiveness. I ask for Your pardon and grace, so that I may live with an innocent heart today and always. Lord, let me be a dynamic example of Christ's love. Amen.

Laborers

"Come to me, all you who are weary and burdened, and I will give you rest. Take my yoke upon you and learn from me, for I am gentle and humble in heart, and you will find rest for your souls. For my yoke is easy and my burden is light."

Matthew 11:28-30

Laborers

Farm workers toil in the
earthen clay, and tromp through
the muddy farmland to try
to save the harvest. Office
workers scurry through busy
high-rises, working to
make their deadlines. Farmers
and office workers feel alone.
Left behind.
Abandoned and burdened.
Humble and in need of prayer.
They are the meek and
humble of heart.
They need our prayers.

Dear Lord,

Help me this morning to be humble of heart. Thank You for reminding all of us who labor with fatigue that You will give us rest. We need to trust in You, for we know that You reward Your followers. Help me to see purpose through all my labors. Amen.

Sungold

"But you would be fed with the finest of wheat; with honey from the rock I would satisfy you."

Psalm 81:16

Sungold

Strands of gold sway in the sun;
succulent kernels burst with wheat.
Honeybees soar from jasmine to jonquil as they
drip with nectar sweet from creation.

Wheat ground in old stone mills, busy with daylight
bread baked in earthen stoves over hot coals
tasty and aromatic, smooth with fresh, creamy butter
that melts on warm yeasty bread and
topped with fresh honey gathered from
waxy honeycomb. Satisfy the hungry
with sweet honey of Your grace.

Dear Lord,

Thank You for feeding my family. I pray that You will feed others. Satisfy their hunger. Let all of Your followers prosper in health and be showered with loving optimism. Dear Lord, help me find ways to feed the hungry in my own life today and always. Amen.

My Prayers to You

May my prayer come before you; turn your ear to my cry.

Psalm 88:2

My Prayers to You

Prayer I give to You this morning, Lord.
My prayers I give to You all day.
Help me remember prayers to thank You.
Not just the prayers that I usually ask.

Dear Lord,

Thank You for Your ear; thank You for Your love and patience.

I ask so much and give so little. Help me know Your love and live Your path to You. Remind me to pray to You, O Lord. Help me to pray to You throughout the day. Help me to realize that You will answer me, but that Your answer may not be my answer. Help me to accept my journey in life and to make the correct choices in my daily journey with You. Amen.

Holy Spirit and Fire

In those days John the Baptist came, preaching in the Desert of Judea and saying, "Repent, for the kingdom of heaven is near ... I baptize you with water for repentance. But after me will come one who is more powerful than I, whose sandals I am not fit to carry. He will baptize you with the Holy Spirit and with fire."

Matthew 3:1-2,11

Holy Spirit and Fire

White mist hovers overhead.
Majestically, white gossamer
paints blue-black skies.

To the side fireballs crackle in
orange, yellow, and red
a blaze to embrace or fear.

White mist, red with fire,
brought by messengers of doves.
Gold letters for minds to decipher.

Dear Holy Spirit,

What wondrous mysteries You unfold before me this morning. Holy Spirit, I repent my sins, and I pray for help so I may be loving and kind. I ask for Your holy fire to envelop every aspect of my life that I may be prepared for the kingdom of heaven. Help me grow in wisdom and grace. Amen.

Love Poured in My Heart

The grace of our Lord was poured out on me abundantly, along with the faith and love that are in Christ Jesus.

1 Timothy 1:14

Love Poured in My Heart

Love has filled my heart,
love sent by God daily. Yet, this
love and grace are not always used in the
best of ways. Help me to be
worthy of Your love, and
to share it tenfold with others.
Love, You pour into my heart.
Help me to have a clean beginning
this morning and every morning,
so that I may live
out Your Word. Amen.

Dear Lord,

Help me to be worthy of Your love this morning. I praise You, Lord, for pouring grace and faith into my life. Let Your offerings overflow in my heart, so that I can share them with those around me. You are astonishing and most admirable of praise. You are the wellspring of all good. Amen.

Hope and Glory

Therefore, since we have been justified through faith, we have peace with God through our Lord Jesus Christ, through whom we have gained access by faith into this grace in which we now stand. And we rejoice in the hope of the glory of God.

Romans 5:1-2

Hope and Glory

Crystal prisms arch in rainbows that
appear in blue morning sky
as I look out my window.

What beauty there is.
Surreal sky, dotted with cotton clouds,
hovers over trees, glorious trees.

Noisy is the chatter of chickadees
as they sing God's gift of nature.
I see His glory and there is hope.

Dear Lord,

Help me this morning to remember to be hopeful and thankful for Your glory. All too often we become hopeless and distraught. This morning, I make a promise to You to be optimistic and show this in my daily life. I will mentor hope for others today. Help my eyes see Your beauty. I pray to You this morning and all day. Amen.

Answers Sought

Why do you make me look at injustice? Why do you tolerate wrong?
Destruction and violence are before me … "Look at the nations and
watch—and be utterly amazed. For I am going to do something in your
days that you would not believe, even if you were told."

Habakkuk 1:3a,5

Answers Sought

Questions, questions I have.
What about this? What about that?
How did this happen? When did this occur?
Why oh why, dear God?
Where am I going?
So many questions.
Quietly, I listen, and wait for answers…
More silence. A lull still surrounds
while anger bubbles,
ready to boil over the black cauldron.
Answers are what I seek,
yet the black cauldron stands over the fire and
reforms itself into a dove, for an instant.
The dove brings water to put out the
fire and soothe the scorch of metal.
For a moment, I realize my answers…
are not Your answers.
Hear my prayers, dear God.
Help remind me to follow Your path,
to seek goodness so that
I will someday understand Your answers.
Let me know that my answers
are not as important as my questions
The pursuit, the questions,
The journey outweigh
Answer's end.

Dear Lord, Help me focus on Your whispers. Amen.

Lonely People

God sets the lonely in families, he leads forth the prisoners with singing;
but the rebellious live in a sun-scorched land.

Psalm 68:6

Lonely People

I watch the beggars on the street with sadness.
Sadness I feel in my belly. Deserted people
with cardboard houses, and no one cares.

Daily they live in their loneliness.
A crust of bread, some garbage remains,
becoming their feast as they eat alone.

Help the beggars and
those alone in cardboard
homes feel Your love, Oh Lord.

Help me reach out to the beggars and the lonely.

Dear Lord,

Today I promise to do something special, something out of the ordinary for a lonely person. Help me to search for signs of loneliness in people so that I can share Your love with them. This morning, I ask You to keep me from going about my life in a nonproductive fashion. Instead, I pray to You for the ability to help comfort and form friendships with the lonely. I pray to You this morning for the lonely. Amen.

Hospitality

He said, "If I have found favor in your eyes, my lord, do not pass your servant by. Let a little water be brought, and then you may all wash your feet and rest under this tree. Let me get you something to eat, so you can be refreshed and then go on your way—now that you have come to your servant."

Genesis 18:3-5a

Hospitality

A gentle man, tired and weary,
took refuge under a tree
while the people that love,
gave him a meal.

His journey continues
after his nourishment received.
The gift of food did help
that weary traveler.

More important, we learn to share
as we gather together
under the shade of
the tree of life.
Help us remember to share
our blessings under the tree of life.

Dear Lord,

Help me to take the time to be hospitable to a friend or to a stranger that I may encounter. Help me to be compassionate to those whom I don't understand. I pray to You for the strength to be an example to those around me by showing Your Spirit through my actions, humble yet firm. Amen.

Justice

Vindicate me, O God, and plead my cause against an ungodly nation; rescue me from deceitful and wicked men.

Psalm 43:1

Justice

Fairness and love.
Forgiveness and hope.
Lead me to the path to true justice.

Help me live as an example
of equality and love around us.
Deceitful and wicked people
tempt us as they touch our lives around us.

Please rescue me
from an ungodly nation.
Help me lead those
around me to the path of justice.

Dear Lord,

I pray this morning that You help me with social justice. There are deceitful men and women all around the world. Please make me aware of the deprived. Help me to focus on Your message so that I can see a vibrant future. Help me bring social justice to the oppressed. Reveal to me a way to bring kindness to those around me this morning and throughout the day. Amen.

Spirit of the Lord

But when the kindness and love of God our Savior appeared, he saved us, not because of righteous things we had done, but because of his mercy. He saved us through the washing of rebirth and renewal by the Holy Spirit, whom he poured out on us generously through Jesus Christ our Savior, so that, having been justified by his grace, we might become heirs having the hope of eternal life.

Titus 3:4-7

Spirit of the Lord

Beauty and grace,
show Your face;
show me the wonders of God.
Spirit filled is my soul, O God.
The Spirit
You have given us.
Help us use Your
gift of grace wisely.

Dear Lord,

Know that I will pray to the Holy Spirit with each breeze of wind that touches my face. Help me honor all of Your creation and to live in Your grace. Thank You for fulfilling the human race with Your Spirit. Please help me to carry out Your wisdom this morning and throughout the day. Help me to spread Your spirit for all to witness. Help me to pray and reflect this morning and all through the day. Amen.

Mercy Request

Do not withhold your mercy from me, O LORD; may your love and your truth always protect me.

Psalm 40:11

Mercy Request

Mercy is what I beg for today.
Do I earn the right to even ask?
To ask to be forgiven and cleansed,
renewed with grace from God above?
Love and compassion, we will love.
Not mere tolerance, we need to give more.
Morning light brings illumination
among the flowers,
prisms of dewdrops
on the blades of grass.
Morning brings
my cry for forgiveness
and the blessings
and grace of Your mercy.
I ask for Your mercy, O Lord
and thank You for Your gift of mercy.

Dear Lord,

This morning, help me live out Your love in ways that best serve Your heavenly kingdom. Protect me with Your love and truth. Help me to show others how Your immense mercy brings love and truth. Help me share Your love and truth with those who do not know You. Help me show them that Your truth is the only truth, and help me share Your love with them even if they do not want to know Your truth. Amen.

Freedom

It is for freedom that Christ has set us free. Stand firm, then, and do not let yourselves be burdened again by a yoke of slavery.

Galatians 5:1

Freedom

Freedom, free this morning.
Thank You for this wonderful gift.
Freedom in the sky; freedom in the clouds.
Free down to ocean depths.
Freedom in the stars.
Freedom for each person.
Goodness, grace, and redemption.
Gifts of free choice
have been packaged to us.
Help me use my freedom
to make the right choice.
Thank You God for freedom.

Dear Lord,

Sometimes I take my freedom for granted. Often, I forget all the pain that people have suffered for the cause of freedom. This morning I thank You, God, for freedom and pray for those who have suffered and died in the name of freedom. O Lord, help me respect and value Your gift of freedom this morning and throughout the day. Amen.

Lift Up the Lowly

"He has brought down rulers from their thrones but has lifted up the humble."

Luke 1:52

Lift Up the Lowly

There they are, the weak,
the tired, the poor, the lowly.
Yet, in their hearts
there are some that
are happy and at peace.

They look to life
with kindness in their eyes.
These peaceful people
share their last belongings with others.

Lift up the lowly
and help me live by their fine example.

Dear Lord,

Please help those considered lowly. I know I am fortunate, but help me to realize that there are those who have been deprived. Help me learn by their example. Most of all, help them find sanctuary in Your arms. Help me to recognize those around me that I could help. I pray for the lowly and all people of the world. Help me find a plan to reach out and help others. Amen.

Spinning Earth

All the earth bows down to you; they sing praise to you, they sing praise to your name.

Psalm 66:4

Spinning Earth

Earth spins around on its axis,
blurs in its journey through time,
toward an end point we know not.

Rainforests, deserts, mountain lakes,
blocks of ice still frozen blue,
oceans of salt water and lakes of clear azure.

Animals hide in forests green,
sleeping in cavernous holes.
Angels journey as earth spins.

Daily we plan our destiny.
Let us sing praise to You
this morning and throughout the day.

Dear Lord,

Good morning. Help me through this day. Today, I praise You and offer my morning song to You. Lord, teach me to praise You in every situation. Give me peace despite bad weather or natural disasters, because You are in control of all the earth. Help me trust You in everything this morning and throughout the day. Amen.

Little Lamb

The next day John saw Jesus coming toward him and said, "Look, the Lamb of God, who takes away the sin of the world!"

John 1:29

Little Lamb

Little fluffy lamb, wooly and warm,
remind us of Your Creator.

Little lamb walking on meadow grass,
bring a smile to the young girl's face.

Remind the girl with golden curls
God made her too. God made all

meadow grass on which You walk. God made you,
wooly lamb. Thank God.

Thank God for all creation.

Dear Lord,

I am comforted in Your flock. You are the shepherd, and I go where You go. This morning, I realize that You gave Your only Son, Jesus Christ, to be a sacrificial Lamb to take away the sins of the world. With this great gift, I ask that humanity be worthy of this momentous act. That we continue to be a part of Your flock, flee from the dark powers of the world, and seek refuge with Your guidance. Amen.

Calls to My Lord

You set aside all your wrath and turned from your fierce anger. Restore us again, O God our Savior, and put away your displeasure toward us. Will you be angry with us forever? Will you prolong your anger through all generations? Will you not revive us again, that your people may rejoice in you? Show us your unfailing love, O LORD, and grant us your salvation.

Psalm 85:3-7

Calls to My Lord

Voices talk over azure sky.
Voices call back and forth;
my voice cries out.
Still no answer.
Perhaps my cry is
not heard.
Then I scream and
beg to be heard.
Still no answer,
at least not heard.
Then I whisper my prayer
and feel a blanket of peace.
Yet, it is not the answer.
I cry out for a response
and receive the gentle breeze of grace.
Help me accept this gift of grace to share with others.

Dear Lord,

Thank You for being so devoted and forgiving. I apologize to You for being so demanding, selfish, and unworthy. Why do I think I am so unique? Why do I think my needs are more important than those of others? Help me to unburden my soul and place my trust in You. Amen.

Awaken

You were taught, with regard to your former way of life, to put off your old self, which is being corrupted by its deceitful desires; to be made new in the attitude of your minds; and to put on the new self, created to be like God in true righteousness and holiness.

Ephesians 4:22-24

Awaken

Awaken this morning, a fresh day.
Spirit within me, begin anew.
Thank You
for this maiden spring light.

Open my soul to
my newly shaped self.
Remind
me to live in goodness
and light. Help me,

Your holiness and Your truth.
Awaken my spirit again
for Your holiness.
Dear God, I thank You for this morning
and every morning.

Dear Lord,

This morning help renew my mindset by removing my old habits and improving myself. Create in me true virtue and sanctity. Make my attitude anew that I may desire to be like You in all aspects of my life. I praise You, God, for Your mercy and willingness to create new life in me. I pray that I would have the humility to accept Your gift of the sacred. Amen.

Lord's Face

And I—in righteousness I will see your face; when I awake, I will be satisfied with seeing your likeness.

Psalm 17:15

Lord's Face

I try to picture Your face, dear Lord,
Your eyes, Your look, Your glory,
How I long to see You.

But for now I must be content
To feel Your love and kindness,
To see Your image in others.

Thank You, Lord for Your face around me.
Help me show respect to others
with each breath I take in the gentleness of morning.

Dear Lord,

I want to see Your face in all its glory, but then I realize You are all around me. I see Your likeness in creation, in a helping hand, in a mother's joy, in the smile on a stranger's face, in the peace You give me, and in the hope You bring me this morning. This morning I feel very blessed and satisfied to see Your likeness around me. Amen.

Love Eternal

Love and faithfulness meet together; righteousness and peace kiss each other.

Psalm 85:10

Love Eternal

Love met faithfulness
eternal.
Righteousness met peace
eternal.
Benevolence we pray for
eternal.

Oh God, help me
Cultivate the cardinal virtues

To share this garden of fruit
eternal.
Help me develop the
Cardinal virtues You gave me.

Help me grow in love and faith
eternal.

Dear Lord,

Thank You for loving me everlastingly. I pray for Your guidance this morning and throughout the day. Please help me live out this day in truthfulness to Your word. I pray that I will be loving and faithful to others and that I would act with righteousness to make peace. Amen.

Hear My Voice

O Lord, hear my voice. Let your ears be attentive to my cry for mercy.
Psalm 130:2

Hear My Voice

Again, I call to You in the forests.
I call out to You from earthen clay.
Here I am Lord, between the trees.
I call to You from the open meadows.
I cry out to You, Lord.
Please hear my voice.
I need Your help Lord.
I ask Your forgiveness.
Thank You for the trees,
and the earth from which
I stand. Oh, dear Lord,
I love You God. For Your
forgiveness, I pray.

Dear Lord,

Please do not abandon me in my hour of need. Help strengthen my voice by strengthening my faith. Give me the capability to manage my life through Your will. My voice is an instrument; give me the notes to form Your music. Help me to ask for unselfish needs, to heed my weaknesses, and flourish my strengths. Hear my voice, Lord. Hear my voice this morning and every morning. Amen.

Morning Glass

Morning Glass

I look out my windowpane of spring glass.
There, a ruffled blackbird perches,
not too thin, and definitely not too plump.
I wonder why the bird is there.

I try to take care of my body, and
fix my morning tea.
There is the bird that stands on a twig
while prettier birds fly around him.

Rose leaves began small, and sprout to
expand a bit more this morning.
Sparrows hop with their usual cadence
to stay clear of the magpie.

Dandelion roots descend once more to
gain a strong foothold in grass that awakens,
each tries to become a weed,
or stay a flower if it should, majestic in creation.

Dear Lord,

The beauty of nature inspires me this morning. I see Your glory in all of creation. Thank You, God, for Your many gifts and the harmony of nature I enjoy this morning. Amen.

Opening Heavens

As Jesus was coming up out of the water, he saw heaven being torn open and the Spirit descending on him like a dove. And a voice came from heaven: "You are my Son, whom I love; with you I am well pleased."

Mark 1:10-11

Opening Heavens

Azure blue skies drift
past moonlit rainbows.
Cascade skies dance to
hues of scarlet and russet that frame
raindrops of amber.
Aquamarine firmament splits open as the dove
flies down on olive branches
to announce His coming.
Praise to God the Holy Spirit.
Praise to You, Holy Spirit.

Dear Lord,

This early morning, I look up at the sky, and it is beautiful. It looks like it is being torn open to show the bright colors of the Holy Spirit. Please remind me that I need to learn to love and accept the Holy Spirit in my life. Help me remember this, and let it be a constant thought and prayer to You this morning and throughout the day. Amen.

Water of Life

Jesus answered, "Everyone who drinks this water will be thirsty again, but whoever drinks the water I give him will never thirst. Indeed, the water I give him will become in him a spring of water welling up to eternal life."

John 4:13-14

Water of Life

Water comes down the mountains.
Rain fills our lakes and streams.
Oceans bring bounty and gifts of food.

Nothing is more important
than the gift of water from God,
the spring of life.

We shall drink from the
spring of eternal life given from God
to nourish and bless us each day.

Dear Lord,

Thank You for the gift of Your water, for it is Your water that will bring us to eternal life. Thank You so much for the spring of eternal life. This morning, help me reflect on this message and grow in love as I seek the true life from Your eternal wellspring. I love You, Lord. Help me to live today as You would want me to live. Help me to make the good choices this morning and throughout the day. Amen.

Glory

But grow in the grace and knowledge of our Lord and Savior Jesus Christ. To him be glory both now and forever! Amen.

2 Peter 3:18

Glory

There is glory in nature;
we find glory in creation,

glory in the heavens above.
Praise God for all we have been gifted.

Always You will be there until the end.
Remind me to live in Your glory.

Do the right thing, and make
honest choices today and every day.

Praise to You, Jesus Christ,
King of endless glory.

Dear Lord,

Please help me grow in grace and in knowledge of You from this morning forward. Help me to find different ways to give You praise. All day I praise You for Your full and endless glory, this morning and always. Praise to You, Lord Jesus Christ. Amen.

Festival

"Amen! Praise and glory and wisdom and thanks and honor and power and strength be to our God forever and ever. Amen!"

Revelation 7:12

Festival

They arrange a festive gathering, and
all rejoice in the Lord.
We honor the saints,
and the angels leading the chorus.
Praise and give glory
in harmony of chords.
I give You prayer this morning.
Gratitude and thanks
are presents to You, almighty God.
Honor and power are Yours.
Please help me to live by Your word,
and Your word alone.

Dear Lord,

Hark! I rejoice and give You my thanks and praises. I am honored to join all the saints and angels in praising You, and I sing joyfully for Your only Son. Lord, I know at times I lose sight of my commitment to You. So for today, I offer my dreams and aspirations in Your holy name, Lord. Amen.

Beloved Son

I have been crucified with Christ and I no longer live, but Christ lives in me. The life I live in the body, I live by faith in the Son of God, who loved me and gave himself for me.

Galatians 2:20

Beloved Son

Jesus was born the son of God.
What does this mean?
How did it happen?
Mystery beyond limits of understanding,
voids occur, streams
do not connect.
Yet, warmth of love touches
hearts. Minds inconsolable,
faith in motion continues to grow, and
nurtures seedlings that
sprout stems of crystal flowers.
Gifts in vases to honor Your Son.
Your Beloved Son.

Dear Lord,

Thank You for delivering Your only Son so that I might be born to eternal life. I surrender my life to You so that Christ may live in me. This morning help me reflect on this truth, knowing it is impossible for me to understand such union. I praise You, Jesus Christ, for loving me and giving Yourself up for my salvation. I pray that I may live my life by faith in You, the Son of God. Amen.

Buttercups and Daffodils

They will celebrate your abundant goodness and joyfully sing of your righteousness.

Psalm 145:7

Buttercups and Daffodils

Daffodils and buttercups unfold
next to bluebells and baby's breath,
beside meadows of wildflowers and green grass.

Clouds drift over the colors with no special pattern;
white textured mist mixes with prisms of light
bordered with an arch of rainbow colors.

God's beauty and creation is bountiful.
Painted heavens open the sky to
find prayers and praise in the beauty of nature.

God shows His goodness
in the drama of creation.
Daffodils, buttercups, and bluebells
remind us.

Dear Lord,

Please help me to enjoy the splendor of nature and all its inhabitants; bright yellows and blues mystify me. Let the flowers of earth serve as a fertile reflection of Your abundant love for humanity. Help me joyfully proclaim Your message of love. Help me to celebrate Your goodness with joy this morning and throughout the day. Amen.

Wings

And God said, "Let the water teem with living creatures, and let birds fly above the earth across the expanse of the sky." ... God blessed them and said, "Be fruitful and increase in number and fill the water in the seas, and let the birds increase on the earth."

Genesis 1:20,22

Wings

Magical whirl of wings
beats so quickly on a bird fragile,
delightful, delicate bird... the hummingbird,
tiny and tenacious.

Unique beauty with grace and speed,
fly by my window this morning.
I stop and pause on my way
to fix morning tea and look out my window
in awe and thanks.

The hummingbird reminds me ...
it is You, Lord, that brought this
symbol of hope, so tiny, so beautiful.
Thank You Lord, dear Jesus,
for all creation.

Dear Lord,

Thank You for this morning. Thank You for the gift of life that You gave me. Dear Lord, I pray to thank You for the world of creatures. Help me learn how to take care of the earth and use it wisely. I will be a good steward. I thank You for the beauty and wonder of nature. Amen.

Grace

For the grace of God that brings salvation has appeared to all men. It teaches us to say "No" to ungodliness and worldly passions, and to live self-controlled, upright and godly lives in this present age, while we wait for the blessed hope—the glorious appearing of our great God and Savior, Jesus Christ.

Titus 2:11-13

Grace

Elusive as the wild orchid,
hiding in the branches
of blue morning light.

White gardenias fragrant
stand in the midst of peonies,
heavy with the weight of grace,

purity, kindness, aromatic with true love.
Help me live in honor and grace
to love the Lord this morning.

Dear Lord,

This morning help me to reflect on my purpose in life. Help me thoughtfully see the light of grace. Help me to love You devoutly in this age of obscurity. Guide me with Your grace toward balance, for this I pray. Amen.

Pain of Shame

To you, O Lord, I lift up my soul; in you I trust, O my God. Do not let me be put to shame, nor let my enemies triumph over me. No one whose hope is in you will ever be put to shame, but they will be put to shame who are treacherous without excuse.

Psalm 25:1-3

Pain of Shame

Shame is such a painful feeling
that pierces through my deepest layers,
and leaves me sad and lonely.

The minute hand reminds me,
arrogance I should not keep.
Let arrogance go.
Make it fly right out the window.

Priorities I must rearrange;
God is the most important.
His relationship I must protect.
It is my duty to make prayer time for God.

Enemies' laughs cannot hurt me.
It is the warm rays of God's sunshine
It is under this glow
That I must live.

Dear Lord,

Sometimes I get too caught up and worry about what others think. Help me to remember that what matters is that I follow Your love and path of righteousness. Amen.

Thankfulness

*Give thanks to the L*ORD*, for he is good. His love endures forever.*
Psalm 136:1

Thankfulness

Thank You, Lord, for the yellow daffodils,
gold and elegant, fragrant and cheerful.

Thank You God for the hummingbird
that dances on the eaves.

Thank You for the fresh pine smell,
piquant and clean to cleanse our senses.

Thank You, Lord, for the minutes this morning
and the minutes I have left.

Thank You, God—I pray to You
today and every day, Amen.

Dear Lord,

This morning, help me remember to be thankful for all the people around me. Sometimes I take people for granted that are most important to me. Help me appreciate each and every person I come in contact with today. Thank You, Lord. Help me to thank them, Lord. Help me to live in Your love that endures forever. Amen.

Morning

God called the light "day," and the darkness he called "night." And there was evening, and there was morning—the first day.

Genesis 1:5

Morning

Blessed are the beautiful mornings
that reflect upon the rising sun.
Beautiful is each wondrous morning.
Joyful are we for all mornings,
thankful for the air we breathe,
grateful for the rising sun.
Mountains reach to touch the sky,
and return the smile of the sun.
Billowy clouds dance,
while dewdrops tiptoe on red flowers.
All unfolds while I make
my morning java, my cup of brew.
I remind myself with each sip of coffee,
I do breathe this morning and that is life.

Awaken my unworthy soul.
Refresh my sleeping senses.
It is my soul and depth of spirit,
not my body that I touch,
and awaken in praise to You
this morning.

Dear Lord,

Thank You for this beautiful morning. Remind me to be thankful each morning for nature's magnificence. Help me to hear Your voice through the morning wind. Help me see and appreciate all of Your blessings, every day. Amen.

God, I Ask for Help

But you, O LORD, be not far off; O my Strength, come quickly to help me.

Psalm 22:19

God, I Ask for Help

Today, God, I ask for help,
help I'll need tomorrow
and again the next day.

Please help me, Lord.
I'll need You tomorrow
and, yes, again the next day.

Thank You for Your assistance.
Thank You in advance.
I need You, Lord, very soon.

Today, tomorrow
and again the next day.

Dear Lord,

Thank You for driving my spirit. I can feel Your help during times of tribulation. Please help me to make the right choices during dubious circumstances. I know that at times, I'm too strident to listen, but I always know that You are by my side—walking with me every step of the way. I continue to be Your dutiful servant, peacemaker, and messenger. Thank You for Your strength every step of the way. Amen.

Perfect Place

When I consider your heavens, the work of your fingers, the moon and the stars, which you have set in place, what is man that you are mindful of him, the son of man that you care for him?

Psalm 8:3-4

Perfect Place

Clouds dot the skies above.
Perfect islands below shade
meadowlands of green grass,
dotted with wildflowers.

Such a beautiful
place that God has given.
Let us use our minds
to live in beauty and respect others.

How great is the work of Your fingers.
Thanks for the moon and stars.
Perfect work of Your creation.
Let us appreciate these heavens.

Dear Lord,

Help me treat Your creation with respect and dignity. I thank You for the heavens and the earth and all the stars that twinkle each evening. These vast creations remind me to praise You for Your abundant love. You take the time to think of me and care for me, even though I am such a small part of Your amazing creation. Amen.

Rejoice

Rejoice in the Lord always. I will say it again: Rejoice! Let your gentleness be evident to all.

Philippians 4:4-5a

Rejoice

Rejoice in the light that surrounds the moon
over a dim sky, decorated with stars that
twinkle, noisy in the quiet night.

Rejoice in the tiny buttercups,
and the song of the large cricket
that makes musical tones in darkness.

Rejoice in your mother and father,
and the life they carry from God.
Rejoice in mankind and your mission to love.

Rejoice in the Lord. He is always near.
I say rejoice. Rejoice in happiness,
and remember to thank the Lord.

Dear Lord,

Remind me to rejoice in You today—to rejoice in all creation. God, the Father, I rejoice in You. God, the Son, I rejoice in You. God, the Holy Spirit, I rejoice in You. I pray to You and offer my day to You. I pray and offer my work to You as I pray in happiness. I pray to You, my Lord and my God. Amen.

Clean Heart

Create in me a pure heart, O God, and renew a steadfast spirit within me.

Psalm 51:10

Clean Heart

My heart is open to think of You, Lord.
Create a clean heart in me.
But what does that mean?
Colors that change in
the chill of the tide?
Soil that darkens
the brightness of red?
What could it be?
Help me, Lord.
Remove the blue chill,
the brown of soil,
the green of jealousy.
Create in me a
clean heart to beat
each moment of my life.

Dear Lord,

Remember that I love You this morning and all mornings. God, help me live with a clean heart that is open to love everyone. Sometimes my heart darkens with unkind thoughts to others. Sometimes I experience jealousy, anger, prejudice, and rage. I need the help of Your grace to create a healthy heart. Renew a steadfast spirit within me and create in me a pure heart; for this I pray. Amen.

God, Our Protector

Hear my prayer, O LORD God Almighty; listen to me, O God of Jacob.
Look upon our shield, O God; look with favor on your anointed one. Better
is one day in your courts than a thousand elsewhere ... For the LORD God
is a sun and shield.

Psalm 84:8-10a,11a

God, Our Protector

God, remember me today, I ask.
Although I am not worthy,
I carry You in my heart, my spirit, my mind.
I try to remember to pray to You each morning.
God, our protector,
keep us in Your grace.
Please give me strength
to follow Your Word,
God, O merciful, our protector.

Dear Lord,

Please protect me on this morning and every day hereafter. Please
protect my loved ones from all harm. I pray to be closer to You, to become
one in spirit with You. I pray for Your grace and strength, so that I may
have the courage to do what is right in the face of adversity. Help me follow
Your path this morning and always. Amen.

Holy Spirit

"But the Counselor, the Holy Spirit, whom the Father will send in my name, will teach you all things and will remind you of everything I said to you."

John 14:26

Holy Spirit

Holy Spirit, please bring the gift of light
to illuminate our souls.
Please bring wisdom to our minds
and joy to our hearts.
Holy Spirit, You are our counselor
and we need Your help always.
Help us grow in wisdom and
in love this morning.
Thank You for the gift of light
to illuminate our souls.

Dear Lord,

Help me remember to pray to You each day. I cannot see You, but I want to feel You in my heart. Watch over me and my family, and help me remember each day to follow Your wisdom, Your truth, Your understanding, Your counsel, Your knowledge, Your piety, Your fortitude, Your reverence, and most importantly, Your love. Help me always to see You in others. Holy Spirit, I praise You. Let us be glorified and adored, together, with the Father and the Son. Let us be one in nature and equal in dignity. Amen.

Curved Morning Path

Many peoples will come and say, "Come, let us go up to the mountain of the Lord, to the house of the God of Jacob. He will teach us his ways, so that we may walk in his paths." The law will go out from Zion, the word of the Lord from Jerusalem.

Isaiah 2:3

Curved Morning Path

This morning I walk along the path that curves
and nature greets me boldly.
Excited songbirds sing to me, and
sit on balmy tamaracks,
while apple trees nod their branches.
Lavender blossoms warm and sweet
color the air with amethyst aroma.
The gentle curve in the path joins a fork,
two different ways to wander.
Help me choose the right path,
to remember the way,
the difficult journey up the mountain
… to God's landing on the peak.

Dear Lord,

Please help me remember to walk in Your path—to climb the mountain of immortality and help others around me to follow Your path. Please let this be my focus for today and always. It is so easy to get distracted with the busy schedule of the secular day and with things that are irrelevant in the scope of life. Help me on this morning to stay on Your path. Amen.

Morning Dove

Make every effort to live in peace with all men and to be holy.
Hebrews 12:14a

Morning Dove

Morning brings white doves,
soft and clean, at peace
sitting on the branch.
Free of spirit they quickly flee, but
one dove returns to her
tender twigs woven in circles,
to protect her young,
gentle dove.
Quiet dove, symbol of peace.
Remind us to live peacefully this morning,
and throughout the days.

Dear Lord,

Thank You for reminding me that You will give me peace, and in peace, I follow You. In today's world, it is difficult to find peace among other individuals. People have extreme difficulty in maintaining peace throughout the world. Help me remember today that my mission must be to live in harmony with my neighbors, family, friends and even those I do not know. Please help me remember that peace is a divine gift from You, O Lord. Amen.

God's Saving

For it is by grace you have been saved, through faith—and this not from yourselves, it is the gift of God—not by works, so that no one can boast.

Ephesians 2:8-9

God's Saving

Our graceful God has shared all gifts with us,
presents to save us all.
Can we accept the packages
gift-wrapped in such a precious way?
We shall love in goodness.
Help us to remember the world of temperance.
Justice is our need.
I pray today in true faith;
Please save me with Your love.
Thank You God
for Your gift of saving grace.

Dear Lord,

This evening, help me reflect on my purpose in life. Please help me to avoid worldly desires that deter me away from my true purpose in life. Help me to love You justly and devoutly in this age of difficulty. I ask Your help to remember this message of Your saving grace, that it may challenge and encourage me to serve You this evening and throughout all days of the rest of my life. Amen.

Sorrow

My eyes are ever on the LORD, for only he will release my feet from the snare. Turn to me and be gracious to me, for I am lonely and afflicted.
Psalm 25:15-16

Sorrow

Pain wounds my heart
and fills my soul with sadness.
Alone, I stand under the stars,
not able to see the moon.

Dear God, I express my sadness;
I give my love to You.
Help me to be worthy of my creation;
help me find my purpose in life.

Dear Lord,

I feel very alone this morning. I try and keep my head up, but I can't ignore my sorrows. Help me to release my distresses, my afflictions, and help me remember to follow Your example. Help me, Lord. Help me to focus on the good of Your creation and on Your infinite goodness. This is my area of focus and help me, Lord, my God. Amen.

Worried

"Then you will call, and the LORD will answer; you will cry for help, and he will say: Here am I."

Isaiah 58:9a

Worried

I toss and turn on cotton sheets;
I cannot sleep. I worry
with many fears that I hide.
Some written on the surface of my
face like crayons. I try to
wash off and cover. My worries
are huge, yet they are tiny. I must
put them in the perspective of what
they are. Tiny specs of dust, not
mountains, towering to crush me.
I lift my eyes to my Savior.
Then I float and relax in my muslin sheets.
Trust in the Lord, I pray.
Then all the world may rest in peace.

Dear Lord,

My worries are always large enough to smother me. Then, I remember that I must trust in You, and You will hear my cry and answer me. I know Your answer will not necessarily be the answer I am looking for, but I must trust in Your wisdom. I pray to You this morning and throughout the day. Thank You for being there for me this morning and throughout the day. Amen.

Abandon

"I will not leave you as orphans; I will come to you."

John 14:18

Abandon

Morning light reminds us.
Darkness does not remain
after night.

Glimmers of light
and hope
warm us each day.

We are not orphans
since we have an eternal Father.
Light for You
will return.

We celebrate
morning light and
give praise to You,
our Father.

Dear Lord,

This morning, help me to reflect on this verse from the Gospel of John. I know that You love me and are always by my side, but at times during the day, I feel abandoned and alone. Help me to feel Your comfort, and remind me that You are the source of all my strength. Help me to trust in You always. I thank You, Lord, for Your blessed consolation on this day. Amen.

Morning Splendor

"I know every bird in the mountains, and the creatures of the field are mine."

Psalm 50:11

Morning Splendor

Splendid blossoms of pink, rose, white,
colorful kaleidoscope of pastel so fragrant,
gorgeous, and succulent. Morning splendor
created by God.

Robins hop in search of breakfast.
Chirping chatter mixes with the melody of songbirds,
harmonious under God's light,
fragrant as honey under the rainbow.

Creator, our God, such morning splendor.
You have presented us morning delights.
It is in the beauty of the mountains
that I see the beauty of creation.

Dear Lord,

Thank You for creating the finery in each morning. I thank You for my beautiful surroundings—green mixed with grand colors and chirping spring robins. Thank You, Lord, for the beauty of spring. I thank You this morning and each morning. Amen.

Lord's Spirit

Therefore, since we have been justified through faith, we have peace with God through our Lord Jesus Christ, through whom we have gained access by faith into this grace in which we now stand. And we rejoice in the hope of the glory of God. Not only so, but we also rejoice in our sufferings, because we know that suffering produces perseverance; perseverance, character; and character, hope. And hope does not disappoint us, because God has poured out his love into our hearts by the Holy Spirit, whom he has given us.

Romans 5:1-5

Lord's Spirit

Spirit of grace above me, a cloud
white and pure, wispy yet opaque,
full of goodness and love.
Help fill me with Your love
so immense and beautiful.
Help me share Your bountiful
gifts with others in my life.

Dear Lord,

Please send Your Spirit out to all peoples in the world so that they may be a living testament of the work of Your grace. Let others see Your love and righteousness. I pray that people all over the world would come to know You and accept Your Spirit. Let them experience Your peace and love. I praise You, Lord, for justifying me through faith, that I may have the blessing of Your love given to me by Your Holy Spirit. Thank You for peace, joy, and hope. Thank You even for the difficulties of my life, because You use these circumstances to build up in me perseverance, character, and hope. Thank You, God. Amen.

Forgotten Wounds

Be kind and compassionate to one another, forgiving each other, just as in Christ God forgave you.

Ephesians 4:32

Forgotten Wounds

A wound I hold deep
within my heart. Actually,
many wounds I save within
my mind and spirit. There
are no expiration dates for wrongs.
My mind remembers wounds I should forget
like a bouquet of wilted
weeds. Help me, Jesus,
to remember Your life
of compassion, and toss
these wilted weeds
to the wind.
Help teach me to forgive.

Dear Lord,

Help me to reflect upon the important passage in the scripture above. I try to remind myself to work at becoming a better person. Please help me learn to be compassionate and forgive everyone that has offended me. I know it is not good to hold grudges and that it only leads to bitterness. Please help me follow Your example, as Jesus has shown in His forgiveness of my sins, so that I may also forgive others in my life. Please help me to forgive anyone who has hurt my feelings or wronged me in any way. Amen.

Jewels

I delight greatly in the LORD; my soul rejoices in my God. For he has clothed me with garments of salvation and arrayed me in a robe of righteousness, as a bridegroom adorns his head like a priest, and as a bride adorns herself with her jewels.

Isaiah 61:10

Jewels

The sun You gave us, our valuable gold.
Night skies, the gift of sapphires.
Abundance of grass rolls as fields of emeralds,
and sunset the present of rubies.
Thank You for all the jewels
You have gifted to us.
Most of all, You gave us love everlasting,
the diamond jewel of love to share.

Dear Lord,

You have given me so many jewels. The jewels of Your creation, nature, and of life around me. Please help me value the most important gift from You—the gift of everlasting life with You. Amen.

Morning Walk of Goodness

I will praise you, O LORD, with all my heart; I will tell of all your wonders. I will be glad and rejoice in you; I will sing praise to your name, O Most High.

Psalm 9:1-2

Morning Walk of Goodness

I walk outside and breathe in goodness.
All God's creation greets me this fine morning.
Red breasts on robins full.
Hummingbirds dart and dance through dawn.
Yellow daffodils with golden brilliance,
spring hyacinths with sweet perfume,
sunrise painted on blue sky canvas.
Paint to perfection palettes
of untold beauty.
Daily miracles beyond my understanding
delight my senses.
I rejoice today, dear God;
I sing Your hymns, O Lord.

Dear Lord,

This morning, I look outside and once again am captivated by Your creations. I pray to thank You for this fine morning. I pray to You that I might notice Your wondrous gifts. Help me to remember that Your gifts of creation should remind me to praise You with all my heart. Amen.

No One Righteous

As it is written: "There is no one righteous, not even one."

Romans 3:10

No One Righteous

Help us remember this important verse.
There is no one righteous,
not even one.

So many times we forget
to be humble, and sometimes
proclaim righteousness over others.

This scripture teaching
reminds us to be humble,
and know our place.

Dear Lord,

This scripture teaching reminds me to be humble and know my place. This passage also gives me comfort in knowing that I am not the only one who falls short of Your holy standard. O Lord, I pray that I would apply these truths to my family and friends, so that I can encourage them to keep walking towards Your plan for waking me this morning and every morning. Amen.

Joyful Singing

Sing joyfully to the LORD, you righteous; it is fitting for the upright to praise him. Praise the LORD with the harp; make music to him on the ten-stringed lyre. Sing to him a new song; play skillfully, and shout for joy.

Psalm 33:1-3

Joyful Singing

Children sing and clap their hands.
Joyful in their smiles.
So excited, their bodies move,
synchrony in joy and glee.

Remind me this morning
of children's delight.
Help me to sing Your praise
today and every day.

Dear Lord,

Let my voice be heard by singing Your harmony. Help me to embody Your innocence by allowing me to adhere to my inner adolescent. As adults, we sometimes complicate our way of living, where as a child, we witness the simplicities of joy. Give me the voice to sing with the children in glee, to sing about You this morning and every day. Amen.

Peace

"Peace I leave with you; my peace I give you. I do not give to you as the world gives. Do not let your hearts be troubled and do not be afraid."
John 14:27

Peace

Such an elusive word in
today's world where different
countries fight and kill and threaten.
We look to other people and wonder …
Why the hatred? … generation to generation?
Passed down from grandparents,
to parents, to children. Let us question
this hatred, this war, this killing.
Help us find a way
to interrupt this cycle
and teach our children love.

Dear Lord,

Help me to lead a very peaceful day each and every day, starting now. Help me to be kind and peaceful until the end of my days. I pray that I handle daily irritations and frustrations with peace, kindness, and justice. Peace and respect of others need to begin at home, within our families. Help me become an instrument of peace this morning and every day. Amen.

Your Spirit

When you send your Spirit, they are created, and you renew the face of the earth.

Psalm 104:30

Your Spirit

Blue is the sky still as quiescent waters.
Silver stones line dry creek bottoms.
Sunrise drifts across the ripples to
wait in patience for the sun.

Slowly we watch and pray.
We ask for Your Spirit above the clouds
to help us understand
the palette of Your landscape.

Refresh and renew. Wait to refresh,
refresh the face of the earth.
Soothe our souls with
the gift of cleansing water.

Dear Lord,

Good morning, Lord. Please send out Your Spirit and renew the face of the earth. I need to feel and live Your Spirit. Help me live out each day, O Lord, in the cleansing water of Your Spirit. Help me to pray to You, Holy Spirit, this morning and every morning. Amen.

Pitcher of Love

And hope does not disappoint us, because God has poured out his love into our hearts by the Holy Spirit, whom he has given us.

Romans 5:5

Pitcher of Love

There the earthen pitcher lay
on the oak table. Full of love,
love that is rich and pure of gold,
honest in its whiteness.

Slowly, each day, the pitcher
of love is poured into
my heart. My heart grows with
richness and warmth.

Help me remember all the
love that God pours each
day to me. Help me
share this love with others.

Dear Lord,

I am not worthy of Your love. This I know, but nevertheless, You pour this love into my heart. Help me accept and honor Your love by showing it to others. As You pour this love from Your pitcher, allow me, in return, to share it with others. I praise You God and the great gift of divine love. Thank You, God, this morning and every morning. Amen.

Holy Trinity

But we ought always to thank God for you, brothers loved by the Lord, because from the beginning God chose you to be saved through the sanctifying work of the Spirit and through belief in the truth.

2 Thessalonians 2:13

Holy Trinity

Three in one. How can that be?
Help me understand this mystery.
I know to seek the Holy Trinity.
Father, I need Your compassion, strength,
and guidance.
Jesus, I ask for Your love, kindness,
and gentleness.
Holy Spirit, please give me Your wisdom,
Your understanding, and empathy.
To be honest I don't fully understand
how three of You can be one, but
I am a humble believer, trying, struggling.
Daily I falter and stumble.
Daily I need Your help.
To You I joyfully pray.

Dear Holy Trinity,

I praise You on this beautiful morning. You are compassionate to me even when I fail You. You love me in countless ways and reveal Yourself to me through different faces. You are my heavenly Father who chose me, personally, to be saved. You are my redeemer, sent to sanctify me and teach me the Truth. You are my merciful friend, hung on a cross to bestow salvation to an undeserving sinner. You are three in one, Almighty God, and I pray that I never forget Your glory. Amen.

Praise

But as for me, I will always have hope; I will praise you more and more.

Psalm 71:14

Praise

I praise You for the morning sunlight,
and I praise You for the chirping chickadees
that play in the sun. I praise
You for the spring daffodils, full of gold.
Thank You for the matching yellow canary
that sings its beautiful song this morning.
Daffodils, yellow and canary gold.
Open our eyes to the sun that unfolds.
I praise You today and forever more.
I praise You each morning
more and more.

Dear Lord,

I praise You now and all day. Every time I see a stunning image of Your creation, please help me remember to praise You for Your creation. Dear God, I praise You and love You now and forever. I will always have hope this morning and every morning. I praise You, my God of love and eternity. Amen.

Rejoice Jerusalem

"Rejoice with Jerusalem and be glad for her, all you who love her; rejoice greatly with her, all you who mourn over her. For you will nurse and be satisfied at her comforting breasts; you will drink deeply and delight in her overflowing abundance."

Isaiah 66:10-11

Rejoice Jerusalem

Rejoice Jerusalem, and all the world sing praise.
Help us to remember to be kind,

to respect every nation.
Let us pray for protection for all nations.

We want to be loving and kind,
respectful and loving, aware of all nations.

Find contentment in all,
for God created all.

Rejoice in God.
Rejoice.

Dear Lord,

During these difficult times in making peace with foreign nations, help us to find resolution. Help us to protect our homeland from the forces of darkness. Let those that are hungry in foreign lands become filled. Let those that are thirsty become quenched. Allow all peoples to rejoice, for once, upon accepting Jesus Christ as their savior, all sinners will rejoice as they come to know God. Amen.

The Spirit and the Dove

But the fruit of the Spirit is love, joy, peace, patience, kindness, goodness, faithfulness, gentleness and self-control. Against such things there is no law. Those who belong to Christ Jesus have crucified the sinful nature with its passions and desires. Since we live by the Spirit, let us keep in step with the Spirit.

Galatians 5:22-25

The Spirit and the Dove

Feathers shimmer under sky-lit clouds.
Humans hover, wait, as the sky opens to show its glory.
Rainbow colors glimmer under bounteous daystar.

Spirit fills the sky to cover the breath of view,
and the dove of peace does appear.

Water cleanses the heavens
with rain, as grace
is able to cleanse my soul.

Oh, Holy Spirit help me
view the heavens in awe,
and seek the peace of the dove.

Dear Jesus,

This morning, I will reflect on the Scripture passage above. Help me live my day today in peace and in love. Help me remember that God wants me to follow the example of His Son, Jesus. Holy Spirit, please help me live this way today, and help me focus on living by Your example this morning and throughout the day. Amen.

Love of God

Though you have not seen him, you love him; and even though you do not see him now, you believe in him and are filled with an inexpressible and glorious joy ... Now that you have purified yourselves by obeying the truth so that you have sincere love for your brothers, love one another deeply, from the heart.

1 Peter 1:8,22

Love of God

Images of love pour in my heart,
dancing in my head
as I hear a whisper.

The whisper is from God,
reminding me of the love
poured in my heart.

I cannot see the love.
I cannot touch the love,
Yet, I feel the love deep in my heart.

Help me share my love.
Help me warm the hearts
of others standing so still around me.

Dear Lord,

I pray to You this morning to thank You for Your love. I honor You and love You. You are wonderful beyond measure, and You give me vast joy. This morning, I pray that You help me share my love for You with others. Help give me the strength to obey Your truth, so that I would be purified and have sincere, deep love for those around me. Amen.

Blessed Be God

Blessed is the man who always fears the LORD, but he who hardens his heart falls into trouble.

Proverbs 28:14

Blessed Be God

God is so good.
He shares His love
with us, the imperfect,
the misguided, to help us.

We are frail and do
not always see.
Our attention is not always attentive,
and cannot always see the love He has given us.

God has shown us,
many times over, the love
that He gives us.
Blessed be God.

Blessed be His Son.
Blessed be the Holy Spirit.

Dear Lord,

God, help me to see Your blessings. Help me to bring You into my day more and more. Help me to share my blessings with the misfortunate. Help me to trust in You each day and to aid my strength and devotion in You. I value You and praise Your glory. I remain Your devoted servant this morning and every morning. Amen.

Lord, I Need to See You

"Hear my voice when I call, O Lord; be merciful to me and answer me. My heart says of you, 'Seek his face!' Your face, Lord, I will seek. Do not hide your face from me."

Psalm 27:7-9a

Lord, I Need to See You

Lord, Lord, where are You?
I am calling Your name
yet, see You, I do not.
It is Your face I want to see.

Where are You, my Lord?
I need to see Your kindness,
the smile upon Your face.
Help me see You this morning.

Lord, it is my faith in You
that guides me
this morning and every morning.

Dear Lord,

Help me to see Your resemblance on all people's faces. Show me that all of Your people are graced with Your likeness, part of their apparel. If I can see humble smiles, I'll know that You have already come into their lives. If I see frowns with tears, I'll know that these are the ones who will need Your touch the most. I pray to You this morning and every morning, God with a human face. Amen.

Shining Light

The people walking in darkness have seen a great light; on those living in the land of the shadow of death a light has dawned ... And he will be called Wonderful Counselor, Mighty God, Everlasting Father, Prince of Peace.

Isaiah 9:2,6b

Shining Light

A glimmer of light illuminates my world today,
A flicker, a spark, what a great light.
Warm my heart and nourish my soul.
Let me see the light in my area of darkness.
Let me reflect in the dawn and remember
these prayers through the sunset.
Help me find the shining light
and walk from darkness into light.

Dear Lord,

You are the light of my life. This morning, I pray that I do not cover Your light with my darkness. Thank You for giving me the light to see. I love You God. Keep me safe and kind, dear Lord, in the hope of Your eternal love. Help me choose the right path to follow You in love, dear Jesus. Amen.

Alabaster Clouds

"You heavens above, rain down righteousness; let the clouds shower it down. Let the earth open wide, let salvation spring up, let righteousness grow with it; I, the LORD, have created it."

Isaiah 45:8

Alabaster Clouds

Fluffy clouds waltz heavy and
mat the sky dense.
Gossamer protects us from what lay beyond
in snug delight.

Help us remember each moment.
Thank You for these billowy clouds.
We give thanks for the gift
of velvet in these drifts.

Softness in our hearts,
white clouds, gray clouds, black clouds.
All gifts from You.

Dear Lord,

This morning I marvel at Your miraculous clouds. I thank You for the gift and intrigue of my environment. Without the fortunate clouds, we would not have the rain to nourish Your fertility. Thank You for using Your gift of rain as a symbol of Your grace, which pours down justice to spring salvation in my life. You shower me with morality so that I may be liberated to Your grace, and feel Your warmth from within. I praise You for what You have raised up in my life and each time I see an alabaster cloud, I will be reminded of Your grace. Amen.

Salvation

The LORD has made his salvation known and revealed his righteousness to the nations. He has remembered his love and his faithfulness to the house of Israel; all the ends of the earth have seen the salvation of our God.

Psalm 98:2-3

Salvation

Sun rises in the sky,
early in the morning.
Frames of pink encircle and drift
over peaks, distant, yet close to our heart.
Through the oceans of time we travel,
reaching nirvana skies high above.
We come face to face with our Maker;
we live in everlasting,
through our chosen salvation.

Dear Lord,

I praise You this morning. You have revealed Your righteousness to me and have made Your salvation known. You have shown me Your love and faithfulness. I ask for the courage to let others know about You. I pray for strength, to stand up for my beliefs, and to share Your love through my actions. You love me every day, and it is my desire that I share Your love with others. Amen.

Morning Light

"For whatever is hidden is meant to be disclosed, and whatever is concealed is meant to be brought out into the open."

Mark 4:22

Morning Light

Good morning, dear God.
How I love You in so many ways.

Here I am in a patch of darkness,
yet, Your will brought darkness to light.

Morning sunrise,
salmon aglow.

How wonderful the twinkle is
in the stars above.

Lord, I see Your cadence.
Let me keep up with You,
let me see Your morning light.

Dear Lord,

I pray to thank You for the morning light that illuminates my thoughts and gives life to Your creation. I want to see Your morning light with my spiritual eyes. I want to appreciate the sunrise and listen to the cadence of nature. Help me to better appreciate the sounds of nature, Your natural music created for us to hear and appreciate. Amen.

Gossip

"Do not judge, or you too will be judged. For in the same way you judge others, you will be judged, and with the measure you use, it will be measured to you."

Matthew 7:1-2

Gossip

A neighbor called to tell me
all about Fred and Sue.
I couldn't believe the stories,
and the awful things they did.
My neighbor did so tell me,
and I told the next three people.
Everyone soon did know,
the terrible deeds of Fred and Sue
until, at last, they lay dead.
How awful I do feel now.
My gossip did destroy
two very good people,
kind souls, Fred and Sue.

Dear Jesus,

This morning, remind me to be like You. As this Bible verse states, help me remember not to judge others, or listen to harsh gossip. It is all too easy to judge others. Please remind me not to make rash judgments, or criticize harshly. I ask for Your help to avoid all gossip today. Help me find the good in each and every person around me. Help me to set a good example and to remind others to discuss the good things about each other, to ask learning questions, not judgmental questions. Thank You, Jesus, and help me to thank others. For this I pray. Amen.

White Clouds

"He draws up the drops of water, which distill as rain to the streams; the clouds pour down their moisture and abundant showers fall on mankind. Who can understand how he spreads out the clouds, how he thunders from his pavilion?"

Job 36:27-29

White Clouds

Fluffy clouds float white as cotton.
Beautiful shapes change and drift.
Sunshine warms my face as I look up in wonder.
Yesterday, I forgot to look up
at the puffs of cotton candy.
Billowy soft against the azure blue.
Calm serenity presented as a gift by our Lord.
Today, the clouds will swell,
and fill with moisture needed
to wet our land, parched.
Today, the clouds will rain.
Our Savior, our Lord, our love.
Remind us, O Lord, of our true purpose.
Help us remember
You each time we
see the clouds.

Dear Lord,

Thank You so much for the gift of clouds and their exquisite beauty and sense of calm. Help me remember that You rained down my Savior, and I must find Your purpose for my life each day. I pray to You this morning and all day. Amen.

Goodness

How can I repay the LORD for all his goodness to me? I will lift up the cup of salvation and call on the name of the Lord.

Psalm 116:12-13

Goodness

When I was sad, Your goodness
comforted me—not right away,
but later, when I recovered
the self-pity surrounding me.
Here I lay in a blanket woven of sorrowful fibers,
meshed together to mask the trueness,
the vision my eyes could not see.
Help me remove this
mask opaque. Release
me from this blanket
so I can see Your goodness.
I praise You Lord
for all Your goodness.

Dear Lord,

Sometimes I am so shallow that I dwell in self-pity, then I focus on clouds to clear my vision. Help me overcome my self-pity and celebrate Your generosity. Give me confidence to call on Your name and proclaim Your gift of salvation. Oh dear Lord, help me praise You in all Your goodness this morning and throughout the day. Amen

Your Servant

Deal with your servant according to your love and teach me your decrees. I am your servant; give me discernment that I may understand your statutes.

Psalm 119:124-125

Your Servant

This morning I awaken,
ready for business and
the items of the day.

I stop and remind myself
to serve, to be Your servant.
I will do Your will, not mine.

Remember the song of the goldfinch
when working to collect material things.
The message is in the songbird's melody,
to ground me in the creation of nature.
A reminder of Your Creation
to learn to serve You, dear Lord.

Dear Lord,

I pray this morning that You will help me be the best that I can be. Lord, I ask that You give me a servant leader's heart. I pray that I can take the opportunities You present to me and serve others every day. Lord, help me have an observant attitude toward things others might ask of me. Amen.

God's Love is Great

For God so loved the world that he gave his one and only Son, that whoever believes in him shall not perish but have eternal life.

John 3:16

God's Love is Great

God's love is great.
Far greater
than my understanding
is His love.
Are we worthy, Lord?
More important—am I worthy?
Your Son came down,
sent by You:
mystical, spiritual, prayerful.
These gifts I need
to thank You for each day.
Help us to not perish.
I pray for eternal life
for everyone in this world.
Now the question remains:
will they accept
this gift from You?

Dear Lord,

Thank You so much for giving us Your only Son, so that I might be born to eternal life by believing in Him. This morning, help me to pray and reflect on this fact that is very difficult for me, a mere human, to understand. Help me follow the compassion lived by Christ. Remind me to follow His fine example so that I, too, may have eternal life. Amen.

Birds of the Air

The birds of the air, and the fish of the sea, all that swim the paths of the seas. O Lord, our Lord, how majestic is your name in all the earth!

Psalm 8:8-9

Birds of the Air

There goes the raven of the night
in all its splendor.
Morning brings the arrival
of the dove in all its peaceful beauty.
Yet, throughout the day, I hear
the chatter of the chickadees
that dance on branches,
the footsteps of the plump robin
as he struts on the grass in pride.
There flies the eagle, the symbol
of our country. I hear the flap
of his mighty wings, and the
whirl of the tiny hummingbird
right outside my window.
How awesome are Your gifts of creation.

Dear Lord,

Once again I am awestruck. Your works are truly majestic in all the earth. Thank You for this psalm, for the birds in the air, and for all that swims in the sea. I praise You, Lord, on this morning and every morning. Amen.

Healing Gifts

Praise be to the God and Father of our Lord Jesus Christ, the Father of compassion and the God of all comfort, who comforts us in all our troubles, so that we can comfort those in any trouble with the comfort we ourselves have received from God.

2 Corinthians 1:3-4

Healing Gifts

Such healing gifts You give us.
Your gentleness, Your kindness,
the touch of wind across my cheek,
Your warm embrace of love,
Your thoughtfulness so gentle.

A lonely old man,
young babies abandoned,
teenagers confused and misunderstood.
Help me to share my time,
help me to understand and love,

I am grateful for Your kindness this morning
and all throughout the day. Let me reach out
and show concern to all those around me.
Let me share Your bounteous gifts,
the many packages You provide us.

Thank You for Your
healing gift of grace.

Dear Lord,

So many people suffer in this world, and I pray for all that suffer. Help me to become more aware of their pain, so that I may reach out to find ways to comfort them. Amen.

Morning Rain

Sing to the Lord with thanksgiving, make music to our God on the harp. He covers the sky with clouds; he supplies the earth with rain and makes grass grow on the hills.

Psalm 147:7-8

Morning Rain

It is sunrise as raindrops glisten
past my morning window pane.

How enjoyable is their dance at dawn!

Succulent hyacinth roots reach
in newly moistened soil.

Spring crocus bow their heads
in the last breath of morning.

Daffodil bulbs wait to unfurl
their yellow buttercups.

As narcissus perfume the
air with intoxicating fragrance.

Herald the life of spring
after the pristine rest of winter.

Dear Lord,

Thank You so much for this fresh morning main! Today I find such joy in nature, which reminds me to praise You for all creation in all its morning splendor and glory. I am thankful for You, dear God. Amen.

Good Morning, Lord

Because of the LORD's great love we are not consumed, for his compassions never fail. They are new every morning; great is your faithfulness.

Lamentations 3:22-23

Good Morning, Lord

Good morning, Lord.
We give You thanks. We praise You
for everything You have done.
Your goodness is wondrous indeed! For
this we thank You. This morning
we look out glass window panes
to see the beauty unfolding,
petals bright and textured,
velvet and luxuriant.
Thank You, Lord, for Your lush flowers.
Most important—thank
You for Your gift
of love and mercy.
This morning help
us share Your love with others.

Dear Lord,

I pray to You this morning to thank You for Your compassion and faithfulness.

Please help me to live each day to give love to each person I encounter. Help me share this wonderful day in celebration with my family, my friends, and everyone I meet. Amen.

Index by Title

144

Index by First Line

148

149

Philippians 4:4-8

[4]Rejoice in the Lord always. I will say it again: Rejoice! [5]Let your gentleness be evident to all. The Lord is near. [6]Do not be anxious about anything, but in everything, by prayer and petition, with thanksgiving, present your requests to God. [7]And the peace of God, which transcends all understanding, will guard your hearts and your minds in Christ Jesus.

[8]Finally, brothers, whatever is true, whatever is noble, whatever is right, whatever is pure, whatever is lovely, whatever is admirable—if anything is excellent or praiseworthy—think about such things.

Index by Bible Verse

New Testament

Design & Typeset Page

This book was designed by Artistic Design Service, Inc. It is set in Adobe Garamond type by Artistic Design Service, Inc. and manufactured by Whispering Pine Press International, Inc.

Adobe Garamond

Claude Garamond (c. 1480-1561) worked to develop the Old Face font Garamond. This font has ha d tremendous influence on the evolution of the typeface developments from the time of its creation to the present. Garamond, or Garamont, is related to the alphabet of Claude Garamond (1480-1561) as well as to the work of Jean Jannon (1580-1635 or 1658), much of which was attributed to Garamond. In comparison to the earlier Italian font forms, Garamond has finer serif and a generally more elegant image. The Garamond of Jean Jannon was introduced at the Paris World's Fair in 1900 as 'Original Garamond', after which many font foundries began to cast similar types. This new interpretation of Garamond, designed by Robert Slimbach, is based on the Original Garamond as a typical Old Face style. However, this font has been expanded to include small caps, expert fonts, and calligraphic caps which were typical of the 15th and 16th centuries.

'Adobe Garamond' is a Trademark of Adobe Systems Incorporated which may be registered in certain jurisdictions.

Reader Feedback Form

Dear Reader,

We are very interested in what our readers think. Please fill in the form below and return it to:

Whispering Pine Press International, Inc.
Your Northwest Book Publishing Company
P.O. Box 214
Spokane Valley, WA 99037-0214 USA
Phone: (509) 928-6038 | Fax: (509) 922-9949
Email: sales@whisperingpinepress.com
Websites: www.WhisperPinePress.com
www.WhisperPinePressBookstore.com
Blog: www.WhisperingPinePressBlog.com

Reader's Name: _____

Address: _____

City: _____

State: _____ Zip: _____

Phone/Fax: ( ) _____ Fax: ( ) _____

Email: _____

Comments/Suggestions: _____

_____

_____

_____

_____

_____

_____

We Invite You to Join the Whispering Pine Press International, Inc., Book Club!

Whispering Pine Press International, Inc.
c/o Morning Reflections
Hood Inspirational Reflection Series – Book 1
P.O. Box 214
Spokane Valley, WA 99037-0214 USA
Phone: (509) 928-6038 | Fax: (509) 922-9949
Email: sales@whisperingpinepress.com
Websites: www.WhisperingPinePress.com
www.WhisperingPinePressBookstore.com
Blog: www.WhisperingPinePressBlog.com

Buy 11 books and get the next one free, based on the average price of the first eleven purchased.

How the club works:

Simply use the order form below and order books from our catalog. You can buy just one at a time or all eleven at once. After the first eleven books are purchased, the next one is free. Please add shipping and handling as listed on this form. There are no purchase requirements at any time during your membership. Free book credit is based on the average price of the first eleven books purchased.

Join today! Pick your books and mail in the form today!

Yes! I want to join the Whispering Pine Press International, Inc. Book Club! Enroll me and send the books indicated below.

Title   Price
1. _____
2. _____
3. _____
4. _____
5. _____
6. _____
7. _____
8. _____
9. _____
10. _____
11. _____
Free Book Title: _____
Free Book Price: _____ Avg. Price: _____ Total Price: _____
Credit for the free book is based on the average price of the first 11 books purchased.
(Circle one) Check | Visa | MasterCard | Discover | American Express
Credit Card #: _____ Expiration Date: _____
Name: _____
Address: _____
City: _____ State: _____ Country: _____
Zip/Postal: _____ Phone: (_____) _____
Email: _____

Signature_____

159

Personalized and/or Translation Order Form

Dear Readers:

If you or your organization wishes to have this book personalized, we will gladly accommodate your needs. (For example: change the names of the characters in a book to the names of the children in your family, Sunday school class, etc.) We can add more information of your choosing and customize this book especially for your family, group or organization.

We are also offering an option of translating your book into another language. Please fill out the form below telling us exactly how you would like us to personalize your book.

Please send your request to:

Whispering Pine Press International, Inc.
P.O. Box 214
Spokane Valley, WA 99037-0214 USA
Phone: (509) 928-6038 | Fax: (509) 922-9949

Name: _____

Address: _____

City_____State_____Zip: _____

Phone: (____) _____ Fax: (____) _____

Email:_____

Language of the book:_____

Please explain your request in detail:_____

_____

_____

_____

_____

Whispering Pine Press International, Inc. Order Form

Gift-wrapping, Autographing, and Inscription

We are proud to offer personal autographing by the author. For a limited time this service is absolutely free! Gift-wrapping is also available for $4.95 per item.

1. Sold To

Name: _____
Street/Route: _____

City: _____
State: _____ Zip: _____
Country: _____
Gift message: _____
_____

Email address: _____
Daytime Phone: (_ _ _) _ _ _-_ _ _ _
*Necessary for verifying orders
Home Phone: (_ _ _) _ _ _-_ _ _ _
Fax: (_ _ _) _ _ _-_ _ _ _

2. Ship To

☐ Is this a new or corrected address?

☐ Alternative Shipping Address

☐ Mailing Address

Name: _____
Address: _____
_____
City: _____
State: _____ Zip: _____
Country: _____
Email address: _____

3. Items Ordered

ISBN # /Item #	Size	Color	Qty.	Title or Description	Price	Total

4. Method Of Payment

International, Inc. (No Cash or COD's)

☐ Visa ☐ MasterCard ☐ Discover ☐ American Express ☐ Check/Money Order
Please make it payable to Whispering Pine Press International, Inc. (No Cash or COD's)

Account Number   Expiration Date
_____ / _____
                                    Month Year

☐☐☐☐ ☐☐☐☐ ☐☐☐☐ ☐☐☐☐

Signature_____
        Cardholder's signature
Printed Name_____
        Please print name of cardholder
Address of Cardholder_____

Subtotal	
Gift wrap $4.95 Each	
For delivery in WA add 8.7% sales tax.	
Shipping See chart at left	
6. Total	

5. Shipping & Handling

Continental US
US Postal Ground: For books please add $4.95 for the first book and $2.95 each for additional books.
All non-book items, add 15% of the Subtotal.
Please allow 1-4 weeks for delivery.
US Postal Air: Please add $15.00 shipping and handling.
Please allow 1-3 days for delivery.
Alaska, Hawaii, and the US Territories By Ship:
Please add 10% shipping and handling (minimum charge $15.00).

Please
By Air: Please add 12% shipping and handling (minimum charge $15.00).
Please allow 2 –6 weeks for delivery.
International By Ship: Please add 10% shipping and handling (minimum charge $15.00).
Please allow 6-12 weeks for delivery.
By Air: Please add 12% shipping and handling (minimum charge $15.00).
Please allow 2-6 weeks for delivery.
FedEx Shipments: Add $5.00 to the above airmail charges for overnight delivery.

Shop Online:
www.WhisperingPinePress.com
Fax orders to: (509) 922-9949

Whispering Pine Press International, Inc.
P.O. Box 214
Spokane Valley, WA 99037-0214 USA
Phone: (509) 928-6038 • Fax: (509) 922-9949
Email: sales@whisperingpinepress.com
Website: www.WhisperingPinePress.com

About the Author and Poet

Karen Jean Matsko Hood began writing as a shy author but has now developed a voice all her own. Her writing always exhibits a unique story as well as a voice of empathy. She is a meticulous wordsmith and combines information with compassion. Hood has been a Christian all of her life. It is only natural that she would channel her efforts to include Christian inspirational books and poetry.

Hood writes about personal and spiritual themes. She also reminds us of the importance of our links with nature and the environment in our daily lives. Hood is passionate both as a feminist and as an active children's rights advocate. She also works to encourage literacy for all ages. Her writing carries the urgency and outrage of current social injustice and inequality. The recurring theme in Hood's work is to provide a voice for those whose struggles cannot be heard. Hood's writing brings hope to the most hopeless of situations. She remains optimistic in her quest for dignity and social justice. Hood's blend of traditionalism and modernism brings a current freshness and poignancy to her own poetic voice. She is versatile in her writing style and is able to incorporate a wide range of themes and topics. Her poems have been published in a myriad of magazines and publications on an international level.

Hood was born and raised in Great Falls, Montana. As an undergraduate, she attended the College of St. Benedict in St. Joseph, Minnesota, and St. John's University in Collegeville, Minnesota. She attended the University of Great Falls in Great Falls, Montana. Hood received a B.S. Degree in Natural Science from the College of St. Benedict and minored in both Psychology and Secondary Education. Upon her graduation, Hood and her husband taught science and math on the island of St. Croix in the U.S. Virgin Islands. Hood has completed postgraduate classes at the University of Iowa in Iowa City, Iowa. In May 2001, she completed her Master's Degree in Pastoral Ministry at Gonzaga University in Spokane, Washington. She has taken postgraduate classes at Lewis and Clark College on the North Idaho college campus in Coeur d'Alene, Idaho, and Taylor University in Fort Wayne, Indiana. Hood is working on research projects to complete her Ph.D. in Leadership Studies at Gonzaga University in Spokane, Washington.

Hood resides in Greenacres, Washington, along with her husband, sixteen children, and foster children. Her interests include writing, research, and teaching. She previously has volunteered as a court advocate in the Spokane juvenile court system for abused and neglected children. Hood is a literary advocate for youth and adults. Her hobbies include cooking, baking, collecting, photography, indoor and outdoor gardening, farming, and the cultivation of unusual flowering plants and orchids. She enjoys raising several specialty breeds of animals including Babydoll Southdown, Friesen, and Icelandic sheep, Icelandic horses, bichons frisés, cockapoos, Icelandic sheepdogs, a Newfoundland, a Rottweiler, a variety of Nubian and fainting goats, and a few rescue cats. Hood also enjoys bird-watching and finds all aspects of nature precious.

She demonstrates a passionate appreciation of the environment and a respect for all life. She also invites you to visit websites at:

www.KarenJeanMatskoHood.com
www.KarenJeanMatskoHoodBlog.com
www.KarenJeanMatskoHoodBookstore.com
www.KarensKidsBooks.com

www.HoodFamilyBlog.com
www.HoodFamily.com

Author's Social Media
Please Follow the Author on
Twitter: @KarenJeanHood
Friend her on **Facebook**:
Karen Jean Matsko Hood Author Fan Page
Google Plus Profile: Karen Jean Matsko Hood
Pinterest.com/KarenJMHood

www.ingramcontent.com/pod-product-compliance
Lightning Source LLC
Chambersburg PA
CBHW021334090426
42742CB00008B/596